BIGGER ISN'T BETTER, BETTER IS BETTER

Cover and book design by Tom Howey

For more information, address:
brad.giles@evolutionpartners.com.au

www.evolutionpartners.com.au

BIGGER ISN'T BETTER, BETTER IS BETTER

Avoiding the pressure for endless growth
to build a better business (and life)

BRAD GILES

To my wife Maggie and my children Mitchell, Reece, Cameron, and Amelie. You continually make me better. Thank you.

Contents

Introduction

You wanted freedom. So why does it feel like a trap?

You're not alone. For 25 years, I've owned and worked with owner-led companies across Australia and New Zealand. And during that time, I've seen the same story play out again and again.

It starts with an owner who's full of life and full of hope. They've built a successful business, often from nothing. They're smart, driven, capable. And yet, despite their success, they feel stuck. The harder they work, the more the business seems to take from them. It's like the bigger they get, the more their life and hope is drained.

I've made the same mistakes. I've chased growth for the wrong reasons. I believed that if I could build a bigger business it would be better, but it wasn't. I've seen those same patterns play out in the lives of hundreds of other owners, people with talent, character and potential, whose businesses became heavier instead of better.

They weren't wrong to grow. Growth is a natural and often necessary part of any business journey. But when the pursuit of bigger becomes the only goal, it quietly consumes the very freedom you set out to create. The business gets more complex, the team gets harder to manage, and the life you imagined, one with energy, space and purpose, starts to slip away.

That's why I wrote this book.

This is not a book about growing a business. There are already countless books that will show you how to do that, most of them written for large corporations. This book is different. It's written for Owner Led Companies. It's about building a better business, not just a bigger one. It's about using the unique advantages you have as an owner to create clarity, rhythm, and structure. And it's about how small, well-directed improvements can compound into something remarkable over time.

This is also not just a business book. It's a personal reset. Because when you're the owner, business and life are not separate. When your business is stuck, your life suffers. And when your personal life is out of balance, your business feels it. There's only one you. And when you're the owner, there's no separating the business from the life behind it. If you want a better business, you need a better life. One fuels the other. That's the work ahead.

Across these pages, you'll find 35 questions — practical, challenging, and focused on the five areas that matter most: a Better Team, Better Customers, Better Offering, Better Financials, and a Better Life, by Design.

I've built over 1,000 business plans with leadership teams. I've seen what works, what doesn't, and what lasts. And I've written this book for you — the owner who wants to build a business that's strong, sustainable, and worth owning.

In my first book, *Made to Thrive: The Five Roles to Evolve Beyond Your Leadership Comfort Zone*, I asked, 'What's the difference between a good leader and a great leader?' In my second and third books about Onboarding I asked, 'How can we reduce onboarding debt and make new hires more effective, faster?' In this book I ask, 'Why do so many leaders in Owner Led Companies chase bigger, only to end up further from the life they really want?'

Let's get started.

CHAPTER 1

What is Bigger? What is Better?

*'They're going back to their offices to find new ways to screw you.
Why? Because they can't help it. They just want to please their boss,
who wants to please his boss, who wants to please his boss.
And they hate themselves for it. But deep down who they hate even
more are guys like you, because you're not like them, because
you don't think like them, because you are different.'*

KEN MILES, FORD VS FERRARI

They're not like you

Just because a company is bigger, it does not mean that it is better.

Moreover, if your company becomes bigger, it does not mean that it will be better.

It does not mean that you will have more freedom, more wealth or you will be happier. If your goal is for your firm to be bigger, and you succeed, it means that it will be bigger. I'm not advocating that you should curb your ambition and have a tiny business; I'm advocating that you channel your ambition to build a better business that delivers you freedom, wealth, and happiness.

You may have already noticed that this book is all about you. It's about you, your family, your employees, your customers. Because this book is written for owners and leaders in Owner Led Companies.

Let's examine why this is important by considering what the media, specifically the business media, discusses.

Firstly, the vast majority of media and business thought leaders talk about corporations. These are often large organisations with enormous advertising and learning budgets that are playing with lots of other people's money. You might read an article about what Google has done or what Walmart failed at, or there could be a book about the things that worked at Microsoft. Most leaders in corporations work for the board, who in turn work for the shareholders, most of whom they don't really know, and who have their own motivations. Also, because corporations have a lot of share-holders, and many are institutional investors, the quarterly report, often muddied with PR, politics and made-up accounting, rules the day. Almost everything in the day-to-day interactions of these corporations is foreign to Owner Led Companies. If you've ever tried to hire an executive or leader from a corporation, you will know how hard it is to have them succeed.

People leading corporations might look like you, but they are not like you.

Secondly, start-ups gain a lot of media attention. Often they gain attention for their meteoric growth or the unusual cultural things they do, like taking the entire team to Las Vegas or providing $5,000 office chairs. Many Owner Led Companies look at these things and think that they can't compete with the perks offered to employees, and that it doesn't make economic sense. And often, it doesn't make sense because many start-ups featured in the media have investors who have provided millions of dollars and are expecting a large, quick return. So, the leaders offer a lot to the people who can achieve this. We work with many start-ups who have wonderful leaders, creating amazing results. There are libraries of excellent books written about start-ups. But start-ups aren't always Owner Led Companies. Start-ups usually have investors who also have their own motivations around growth and quarterly performance, and that, often, also rules the day.

Third, we have Owner Led Companies that the media largely ignore. Leaders of Owner Led Companies aren't accountable to someone in the way corporations and start-ups have shareholders and investors. Maybe they have a few investors or shareholders, but generally, the people leading the company own enough of the company that they don't answer to anyone. This might be greater than 50 per cent individually or as a voting block, or it could be as high as 100 per cent. The owner could be the CEO or the chair, with a CEO running the day-to-day business. Amongst the thousands of Owner Led Company CEOs I've known, I've found the freedom of not having a boss to be the single largest motivation to work hard, but also, this freedom is the single largest cause of success and failure.

In this sense, corporations and start-ups have more in common with each other than they do with Owner Led Companies. This simple accountability mechanism, where most shareholders don't work in the business yet set the objective for a particular result, can be extremely effective. Eventually, everything corporations and start-ups do 'should' connect to shareholder value. Theoretically, if it doesn't add value, then the employee, CEO, or board member loses their job. It's a simple equation. As a shareholder, it's a useful tool to motivate the team, maintain discipline, and have everyone aligned toward the same goals.

But Owner Led Companies don't have that external mechanism. They work for themselves. They don't want a boss and probably would struggle to work for one. They value freedom. But their freedom, your freedom, comes at a cost. Just like the long-term prisoner who leaves jail and struggles without the discipline of prison life, we can all struggle without the discipline of accountability.

Those who aren't running an Owner Led Company might sound like you, but they are not like you.

The Problem with Freedom

If someone else sets your objective, and that objective is something such as shareholder return or valuation growth, you'll draw a line to that and 'mostly' ignore everything else. This will be the focus of your efforts. However, if you are free and no one else sets your objective, there are endless possibilities. There isn't one path you must take; there are countless paths you could take.

Without the discipline of external shareholders or investors to set your objective, your one path, you can become undisciplined. Indeed, this is why the entire industry of personal trainers and business coaches exists: to hold people accountable.

Without a single path, we often try many paths. We head down a path, trying a new initiative, method, or effort, often inspired by corporations, until we feel that path isn't the right path for us, and so we try another path. Over time, we can become frustrated or impatient that our ongoing search isn't providing a focus for our efforts.

As an entrepreneur, you can do anything. But you can't do everything.

As a mentor of mine once said, *'The problem with entrepreneurs is that the profit doesn't stick'.*

The problem with freedom in Owner Led Companies is that despite all the great things freedom brings, and there are many, the company can end up with an undisciplined, impatient leader, who is an impulsive risk taker.

To build a better business, we must be patient and resist the pressure for endless growth - the undisciplined pursuit of more. We must be disciplined to execute the short-term objectives such as profit and revenue. And we must be both disciplined and patient to consistently execute milestones toward our longer-term objectives.

Let's take a look at what happens when we consider discipline and patience as attributes for the leader of an organisation in Figure 1.1:

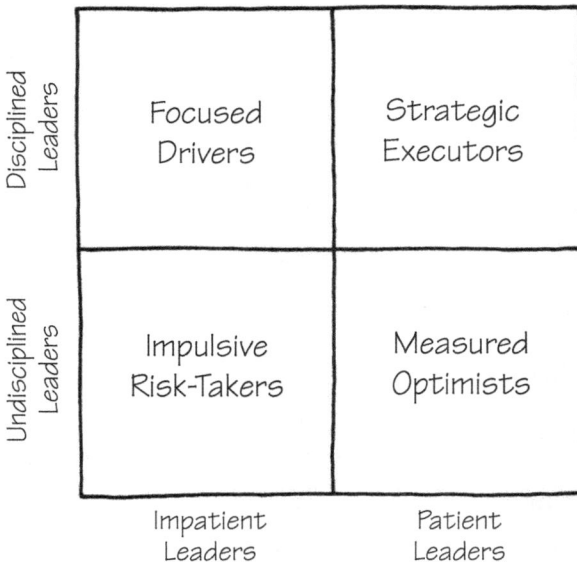

Figure 1.1 **Discipline versus Patience in Owners**

On the vertical axis in Figure 1.1, we have undisciplined and disciplined leaders. On the horizontal axis, we have impatient and patient leaders. Let's consider the labels in each quadrant and what they mean.

Impulsive Risk-Takers (Impatient and Undisciplined Leaders)

Impulsive risk-takers are quick to take action and can achieve occasional successes through bold, fast decisions. When opportunities rapidly arise, especially in the early days of a company, an impulsive risk-taker can bring great value. The challenge occurs when Owner Led Companies begin to normalise, and the leader can become bored while the business desperately needs longer-term plans and direction. The impulsive risk-taker can prioritise short-term gains at the expense of long-term strategy and sustainability, which can lead to over-committing financial and personnel resources, thereby weakening their organisation. The freedom that offers countless paths to the leader can trap them in this quadrant for decades.

Leaders who don't evolve to increase their discipline and patience will quickly find that these traits work against their real objectives.

Focused Drivers (Impatient and Disciplined Leaders)

Focused drivers propel the business forward efficiently, delivering swift results with accountability, making them highly results-oriented. When a company needs short-term results, such as restructuring or after a crisis, a focused driver might be necessary. However, in a normalised business, focused drivers can prioritise immediate results over long-term goals. This can lead to impulsive decision-making that sacrifices long-term strategic objectives for short-term gains. A successful strategy requires careful planning, analysis, and consideration of various factors. The focused driver may rush through the strategic planning process and not have the patience and persistence to execute a successful strategy over many years, especially if they do not see immediate results.

Disciplined leaders who don't evolve to increase their patience will find they can burn out employees with their unwavering focus on shorter-term goals and fail to successfully execute a longer-term strategy to differentiate their company from the competition.

Measured Optimists (Patient and Undisciplined Leaders)

Measured optimists can build an excellent long-term strategy considering all the critical factors to differentiate and execute. When a business is more concerned with building for tomorrow rather than today's results, measured optimists can be very useful. However, their lack of discipline can lead to poor execution of strategy, undermining their usefulness. Equally, as a business leader, measured optimists can struggle to get team members to succeed, lacking the discipline required to hold others accountable and being far too patient with staff, hoping they will self-correct and create the necessary results.

Patient leaders who don't evolve to become more disciplined can get caught out when they neglect the core business and its related cash flow for other longer-term, exciting opportunities such as new products or new businesses. The neglected core business can then become unprofitable and cascade into larger issues.

Strategic Executors (Patient and Disciplined Leaders)

Strategic executors possess both the discipline and patience to develop an effective strategy and vision, carefully plan their actions, and successfully execute over time, resulting in steady progress and sustainable growth. Strategic executors have the discipline to hit short-term financial targets and priorities. They also possess the patience to pursue longer term strategic milestones that can take years to implement before the business secures a unique, valuable position in the market. Strategic executors find a balance between financial stability today and organisational viability and evolution into the future.

In times of crisis, strategic executors may need to become more like focused drivers, postponing strategy execution to stabilise the company.

To escape the problem freedom creates when too many paths appear, entrepreneurs and leaders in Owner Led Companies must evolve from undisciplined risk takers into strategic executors so their effort counts for the most and ultimately delivers freedom, wealth and happiness. Building a better business starts when the owner leader recognises that growth pursued without discipline and patience might get you bigger, but it will never get you better.

What is Bigger?

Bigger is about wanting to be bigger for the sake of being bigger.

Bigger is the voice inside your head saying that if you get to $100m in revenue and the business is ten times bigger, then you will be a big shot.

Then people will respect you. Then you will be adored, or you won't have to do what you're told. Then you will impress your parents, friends, neighbours, or the people you don't care about at all.

The subconscious reason you are drawn to bigger is because bigger is exactly what your ego wants.

Ego is your worst enemy. It's weak and frail and emotional. It's clouding your judgement when it uses emotion to tell you that, in fact, yes, *bigger is better*, and it draws you to that belief like a moth to a flame—not really knowing why you're going to the flame, not knowing what will really happen once you get there.

Ego isn't concerned about risk. Ego allows you to become wrong or complacent or distracted or weak. Ego gives you bad feedback, disconnecting you from reality. Ego is defensive at a time when you cannot afford to be defensive. Ego tells us that our success to date has been due to our unique talent rather than the grinding hard work that really happened. Ego tells us that our talent alone is enough to easily do something bigger, without the hard work it takes to get better.

If you reach $100m in revenue or are well past that, then I couldn't be happier for you. But as Alan Miltz said, 'Revenue is Vanity, Profit is Sanity, and Cash is King.' No matter where you are, better is always better.

We set Big Hairy Audacious Goals or BHAGs® - a ten to thirty-year goal defined by Jim Collins - with leadership teams all the time. Of course, by definition, they're big and audacious. However, they must be informed by strategic logic and, therefore, an understanding of how to get there. That prior strategic logic and understanding tells us how to build better, so the BHAG® will logically result from that work.

Better companies will grow because they are better. They focus on being better and may grow to become bigger as a result. Companies that chase being bigger tend to focus on doing more, rather than on what they can be the best at.

As Jim Collins says in his book *How the Mighty Fail*, 'Once an organisation has achieved some success and hubris has set in, the Undisciplined Pursuit of More catapults a firm toward decline and failure.'

As Collins says:

'*Hubris leads to the Undisciplined Pursuit of More—more scale, more growth, more acclaim, more of whatever those in power see as 'success.' Companies in this stage stray from the disciplined creativity that led them to greatness in the first place, making undisciplined leaps into areas where they cannot be great or growing faster than they can achieve with excellence, or both. When an organisation grows beyond its ability to fill its key seats with the right people, it has set itself up for a fall. Although complacency and resistance to change remain dangers to any successful enterprise, overreaching better captures how the mighty fall.*'

And so an undisciplined leader of an Owner Led Company might suffer from hubris borne of their previous success and might be impatient to succeed. We then create the recipe for an impulsive risk taker to overreach with big bets. The formula is set to focus on bigger.

About twenty years ago, I won an award from the country's leading business publication for being the eighth fastest-growing company in Australia. I bought into the philosophy that bigger is better and the faster, the better. Most of the less-than-complementary things above could have been written about me then. But that publication wasn't writing about companies that were better; they were writing about companies that were fast growing because that was abnormal. Because that's what sells magazines and advertising.

But the myth that fast growth is best is indeed a myth. When Dr. Gary Kunkle joined me on my podcast, he explained that fast growth radically decreases the odds of survival when supply runs ahead of demand and is funded through debt. As the former economist at *Inc.* magazine and now part of the Tugboat Institute, Dr. Kunkle emphasised that growth should be funded through earnings, not debt, and that supply should match demand. This might mean your growth slows, and maybe you become better, not bigger. But the first rule of business is that you must survive.

As shown in Figure 1.2 and Figure 1.3, when a business has more sales than it can handle, demand is ahead of supply. Naturally, most entrepreneurs will want to invest in increasing capacity to meet that demand. But increasing capacity doesn't guarantee that sales will stay at the same level or keep growing. You might call this 'build it, and they will come'. When that increase in capacity is fuelled by debt, you might have gotten bigger, but you've also radically reduced your chances of survival.

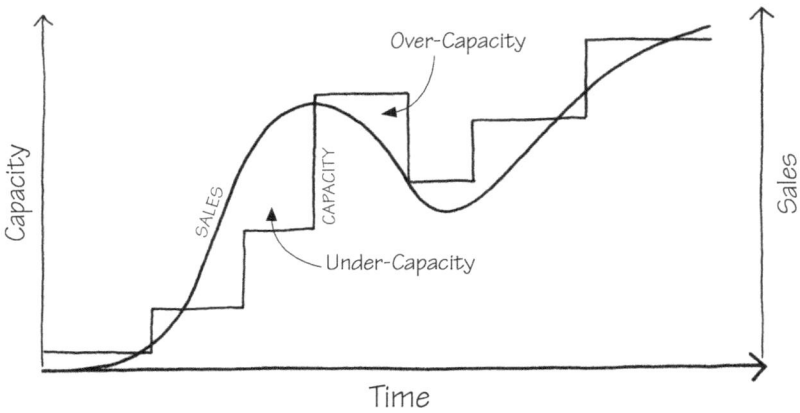

Figure 1.2 **Matching supply and demand** *Adapted from Dr Gary Kunkle*

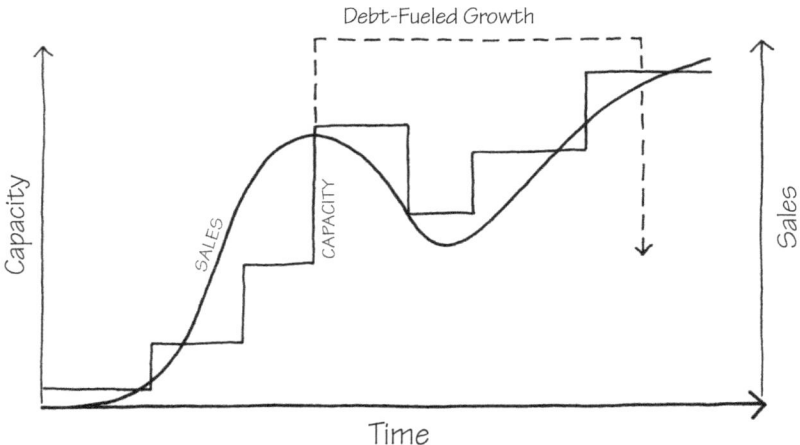

Figure 1.3 **Matching supply and demand with debt** *Adapted from Dr Gary Kunkle*

Lou Holtz, the American football coach, is quoted as saying, 'In this world, you're either growing or you're dying, so get in motion and grow.' That's surely motivational, but how do you interpret that statement? Most small to medium business owners would probably react to that quote by saying, 'I must grow revenue.' But there are other things that you can grow, for as we know, revenue is vanity. Revenue is easy, and bigger revenue can end up being terribly expensive. In writing that last sentence, I instantly think about a company offsite planning workshop I facilitated a couple of weeks ago where the CEO said to his leadership team, 'Revenue will cover up all our problems.'

The root cause of those problems is that:

The company doesn't have a strategy that differentiates it in the market and meets its customers' needs. It lacks genuine customer loyalty.

The business's leadership and management are full of reliable stewards, casual dreamers, and mostly indifferent observers (see Chapter Three for a description). It's friendly, and people try hard, but the business isn't run by curious achievers, people relentlessly in pursuit of their goals.

The business owner is undisciplined and impatient. He is an impulsive risk taker surging from thought bubble to thought bubble, desperately trying to get enough revenue to cover the ever-growing expenses in a tumultuous world and eke out a profit.

We've done some great work to turn this situation around, but those root causes have been there for decades and many of these things tend to calcify.

In another leadership team, I vividly remember a 2-day workshop that a part owner in the business attended (out of courtesy more than anything). I recall their answer to every question was, 'Do more deals'. 'How could we be different?' I asked. 'Do more deals'. 'What's our profit per X?' 'Do more deals'. 'What's the most important thing we've got to do in the next year that's not related to the number of deals?' 'Do more deals'. You get the picture. Much like the first CEO above, this leader had his own version of the belief that 'revenue solves our problems'.

Like any drug, once you get addicted to revenue growth and it becomes the answer to most problems, you become a slave to it. The more you focus on revenue growth at any cost, the more it will cost you.

What is Better?

Better is a choice.

Better means shaping your business so it enables you to live your one-and-only life in the most rewarding way possible for you and the people you love.

Better is about building a better life—not just financially, but across the areas that matter most: your health, your family, your happiness, your growth, and your freedom.

Better is about building an asset that grows your wealth, where that asset works for you.

Better is about having a business that excites you, that challenges you and that you enjoy participating in.

Better is about being intentional with your effort.

If you focus on becoming bigger, there is no evidence that you will achieve the above. Much of the time, focusing on bigger actually achieves the opposite of the list above.

But the irony is that when you focus on better, you often end up with a bigger business anyway, and along the way you grow your freedom, your wealth, and your happiness.

When I interviewed Bo Burlingham, former executive editor of *Inc.* magazine and author of *Small Giants* and *The Great Game of Business*, on my podcast *The Evolution Partners*, I asked him how he defines a better business. He replied: *'What kind of experience are they having? What kind of experience are the employees having, the customers and the suppliers? So if all those people are having a positive experience, they feel the loyalty to that business. And then they are inspired, and that business inspires the people who work for it, the people who supply it, the people who buy from it, and the other people outside in other businesses who look at it and say, that's the kind of business I wanna have.'*

Then, when I asked the financial guru Greg Crabtree, author of *Simple Numbers* and *Simple Numbers 2.0*, he replied, *'When you're talking about running a better business, I've got to be able to stay in the game and then take advantage of when the game allows me to gain.'*

Also, I asked Allan Dib, the author of the *One Page Marketing Plan* and *Lean Marketing*, who replied, 'A *better business begins with the owner, who must answer the question "what am I optimising for, what is the outcome I want?"'*

These themes are common amongst the thinkers, planners, and doers I talk with on the podcast. When I introduce the concept that bigger isn't better, almost everyone I speak with pauses agrees with the concept and provides their perspective, which tends to fall within similar themes as I've arranged throughout the chapters in this book.

In my book *Made to Thrive*, I outlined the five key roles a CEO must fulfil for a company to achieve great results, not just good ones.

These five results are:

Higher percentage of top performers

Top performers, the top 10 per cent within an industry, are attracted to working for great CEOs who produce better results. These highly motivated and driven employees simply *can't* work for leaders they don't view as great. They might tolerate a good CEO, but only until they can find a better leader to join. They know a CEO who isn't great is impacting their career and are acutely aware that they want their potential to count for the most.

Higher retention

Great CEOs are good role models and positively impact culture, causing employee engagement and satisfaction scores to rise. Subsequently, employees tend to stay longer as great CEOs provide less reason to leave.

Higher productivity

Great CEOs get a higher return for each dollar paid to employees. People in the organisation are more effective because a successful strategy generally produces a higher gross profit relative to their compensation, and an attractive culture is conducive to a more productive environment.

Consistent growth

You can bank on a great CEO growing the business every quarter and every year. The efficacy of strategy, its ability to drive revenues and profits, and its ability to actively consider all potential growth-affecting issues ensures that growth occurs no matter the environment.

Consistent results

There are no surprises with great CEOs. They have successfully mitigated risks and built a group of employees and suppliers who do what they're supposed to do when they're supposed to, achieving the goals they set and producing the expected results quarter after quarter.

And so, if an Owner Led Company seeks to become better, what does a better business look like?

A better business must inspire its people. It should energise the owners, leaders, employees, customers, suppliers, and even those watching from the outside.

A better business must earn loyalty. It must create real connection with customers—so they trust you, stay longer, and become advocates.

A better business must focus on what it can be the best at. Trying to grow by offering more products or services that are only good—but not great—is just scaling mediocrity.

A better business must be financially strong. It needs the discipline, structure, and operating system to survive tough times and deliver consistently strong returns.

And a better business must not drain the energy of its owner. The biggest energy drains come from poor planning, poor strategy, and the absence of a system to run the business.

In the end, a better business is one that gives more than it takes—so you can build not just a better company, but a better life.

If you can keep three simple measures in the green year after year, your business will compound. I call this the 15-15-15 model, a simple, powerful way to measure whether you are building a better business. The goal is to consistently achieve:

- *More than 15% annual revenue growth — fall below this and you likely do not have a strong enough strategy.*

- *Less than 15% annual employee attrition — exceed this and you probably have cultural or leadership issues to fix.*

- *More than 15% profit — drop under this and either your business model needs work or your execution must improve.*

Each is interdependent. You might be profitable and have low attrition, but without revenue growth, you cannot compound. You might grow quickly and have low attrition, but without profit, the growth is not sustainable. Or you might grow revenue and profit but burn out your people, which erodes performance over time. Keep all three green year after year, and you create the kind of sustained compounding that defines a better business..

As outlined above, to build a better business, we must transform an undisciplined, impatient leader from an impulsive risk taker to a strategic executor. For entrepreneurial doers, this can be quite challenging but necessary once they discover their real goals. We do that by embedding a management and leadership operating system that increases discipline and patience, surrounding the leader with a framework to build a better business.

It's hard to avoid the temptation of bigger and instead focus on better when we live in a world geared toward bigger. And that's what we're going to talk about in the next chapter: the pressure we all face to chase bigger.

CHAPTER 2

The Pressure for Bigger

'The first principle is that you must not fool yourself–
and you are the easiest person to fool.'
RICHARD FEYNMAN

Vanity or Sanity

We live in a world of effort.

Every sports win, every business achievement, every academic accolade, every creative pursuit is linked to the human need to achieve. And they all require enormous amounts of effort. Having written a few books myself, I'm astounded when I walk into a library and contemplate the effort that's gone into each book multiplied by the number of books on the shelves.

Those who don't put in the effort do nothing, achieve nothing, and get nothing. There's an underlying fairness to life in this respect most of the time. Sure, there are people who inherit wealth or success, but for many of these people, the gift they get can become somewhat of a curse. They end up with a void inside that can't be filled. They haven't truly challenged themselves.

In reflection, the human struggle doesn't ask, 'What did I receive?' it asks, 'What have I done?'

So don't envy what you didn't get or what others have received, for this could actually be a burden, a white elephant that takes away the true reward of your life.

Instead of envy, hope that you have a life where you were challenged. Hope to live a life where you built something meaningful to you. And through that journey, you overcame the challenges that life could throw at you. Hope for a life where you achieved what you wanted to.

But the problem when pursuing achievement in the business world is that we don't know how to win. We know when sports teams win. When they win the game, the team knows it, the opponents know it, and the fans know it. And that's the end of the story. Maybe the win on that day forms part of a championship, and a bigger goal is to win the grand final for that year. Nonetheless, the objective is still clear. Score more points than the other team in the allocated time.

We can think in the same way across other areas of human endeavour. For example, in academia, the 'win' might be publishing a peer-reviewed paper or becoming a tenured professor. In creative pursuits, it might be the release of a song, movie, or play.

In each of these areas, we're aware of what winning means. The game sets the rules. A part of being a successful book author is publishing a book. A part of being a successful sportsperson is competing and winning in your chosen sport.

But business is different. Business doesn't have rules in the same way a sports game does. Sure, in business, you must adhere to the law, and there are ethical considerations, but there are no points on an agreed scoreboard like in sports. The definition of the competition is subjective, and the time never ends.

And so very quickly, business leaders can slip into a vortex of meaning. They might subconsciously think;

'I exist in a world of effort, and I commit my effort to succeed in business.

To exist in business means that I must participate in a market to sell my goods and services alongside others who are trying to sell to the same customers.

Therefore, this must be the game.'

But this 'game' has no rules, no defined score, and no actual definition of winning. As humans, we're hardwired to compete and to achieve, so we try to understand what it might mean to win in the game of business.

Perhaps it's opening an office in another city or another country.

Perhaps it's reaching $100 million in revenue.

Perhaps it's owning a sports car or a private jet.

Perhaps it's market share or being larger than a competitor who annoys you.

And these might be worthy goals for you, but they don't define the game of business. I've worked with clients who have achieved these, and it's not the same as holding the premiership cup aloft at the end of the sports season.

Ask a sportsperson what success looks like, and they might say winning the premiership or grand final. I've asked hundreds of entrepreneurs this same question, and the answer is often something like:

- *A fleet of 50 work vehicles, or;*

- *An office in each state or;*

- *100 employees*

However, these definitions of success are all expenses within their financial statements. My reply would be that we could buy those expenses today if we went into enough debt. If you similarly define success, even subconsciously, it might mean you're chasing the wrong goals. I recently discussed this with an entrepreneur I work with, and he told me that when you read the annual reports of his competition, which he can because they're on the stock exchange, it's full of highlights about their expenses. It's full of photos of the number of machines they have, their expansive offices across the country, and a group photo of all their staff. And that's not just one competitor. It's the whole industry showing off in the same manner. People in that industry feel the pressure to show off their expenses.

What would be an alternative?

- *Here's a photo of machine 41. Thanks to our Singapore team, it's operating at 2.1 times the industry average.*

- *Here's a photo of our Auckland office. The team in this office have a revenue per employee 45 per cent higher than the industry average.*

- *Here's a photo of our innovation winners for the last year. Collectively, they have added $4 million in profit with ideas to reduce waste and improve gross profit from our products.*

Maybe you're reading that and thinking, 'I'm not that silly! I wouldn't chase expenses like those others', and if asked, you would say a revenue number, like $30 million or $100 million. That's what success would look like to you. In some ways, defining success as a revenue number is worse than having your definition of success as an expense.

As the financial guru Alan Miltz said, 'Revenue is vanity, profit is sanity, and cash is king'. So, your $100 million could be a vanity project. A very expensive vanity project. I remember 18 years ago, in another company I owned, one of our main competitors was publicly listed and turning over about $100 million, roughly ten times our revenue. And, of course, because they had to report to the market, we could see their results and strategic plans. Even though their revenue was ten times ours at that point, we were making almost ten times their dollar profit.

Their revenue was just under $100 million, and they made around $100k profit.

Our revenue was just under $10 million and made just under $1 million profit.

In the same way that you can buy expenses if that's how you define success, you can also purchase revenue if that vanity metric is how you define success. If you have a laser-focused desire to build a business with $100 million in revenue, then we can get you there, no problem. The only question is, how much can you spend to get there?

- *It will cost money to hire A players.*

- *It will cost money to acquire businesses.*

- *It will cost money to open new locations.*

- *It will cost money to build new products or add inventory.*

- *It will cost money to implement suitable systems and processes for your new size.*

But again, these are just a few of the expenses required to achieve the $100 million revenue definition of success. So, it's almost like you've defined success as an expense.

This is simply a math problem. If the cost of growth exceeds the cash that the business can generate and reinvest into growth, then that shortfall must be funded. Put simply, if it costs $750,000 to open a new location and your business doesn't have that money on hand, you either don't open it or you have to find a way to fund it.

If you have that money, or the bank will lend it to you, or you find shareholders to provide that money, you can pay to open the new location. And that location might produce $1 million in revenue. There's still $99 million in revenue to achieve your $100 million goal. At this rate, you must find $74,250,000 to fund the remaining locations.

Imagine that you somehow find a bank that will loan you $74 million. And you open new locations and get to $100 million in revenue. Congratulations! If you manage to achieve a 10 per cent profit, you now have a $10 million profit. But, at 7 per cent interest plus principle on a ten-year loan, you're paying $10.3 million in repayments per year. Of course, there are also taxes, working capital and a range of other things to pay but put simply; the paper napkin math won't work. 'Yeah but I'm smarter than that' you might think to yourself. 'I will sell it once I hit $100 million'. Assuming you sell your business for four times the EBIT profit (a typical valuation), you've just agreed to sell a '$100 million business' for $40 million, and have $74 million in debt. Of course the bank wants its money first, so you must give them the whole $40m, and you're left with no business and $34m in debt. You're financially going backwards when you achieve your bigger goal. You're paying the bigger price.

Maybe the pressure to achieve bigger pushed you to set a goal that wasn't really that considered or planned properly and might not be what you really want. But also, if you get there, what have you sacrificed, and how much has it personally cost you to get there?

Without a clear definition of how to win, we are at the mercy of our psychology, our DNA and influences from the outside world. Or, put another way, the way we think, the way we're made and the society we're surrounded by. These can be brilliant, driving and aligning us exactly where we need to go. But more often than not, they can lead to years of misplaced effort, with leaders trying to win a game that you can't really win at all.

The Pressure for Bigger

Your psychology

Your life experiences, beliefs, and emotional wiring all shape the way you show up in business. But to truly understand the pressure for bigger, we need to look beneath the surface and explore the internal drivers that shape your decisions.

Where does motivation come from?

Imagine two people competing to win a deal. The first is experienced, looks smart, and asks all the right questions. Their pricing is sharp. There is no reason they shouldn't win the deal.

Then, imagine a second person. Everything is exactly the same as the first person, but they are more motivated to win. They conduct more research than the first person, and they more deeply understand the motivations and decision-making in the customer's firm. They're not only meeting with the point of contact but with all the decision-makers and influencers involved in the decision. It's taking more time and more effort. They are hungrier.

The second person is prepared to sacrifice more to succeed. This is true in every situation in life. Different people are prepared to sacrifice differing amounts to achieve, depending on how important something is to each of them.

Consider Figure 2.1, anecdotally representing the population across five segments through a bell curve.

- *Firstly, a very small percentage of people aren't willing to sacrifice anything to achieve what they want. If they need to sacrifice anything at all, they don't want it. They want the world handed to them on a plate, and they want the plate to be brought to them.*

- *Next, we have a small percentage of people who are willing to make a small sacrifice to achieve what they want—just a little bit of sacrifice, but not much at all. These people might be long-term unemployed, or if they have a job, they expect the employer to continually sacrifice more so they can get what they want.*

- *The vast majority of people, perhaps two-thirds, are willing to sacrifice in order to achieve what they want.*

- *Then there is the small percentage of people who will sacrifice almost anything to achieve. They work all night and on weekends, putting their goals before family, health, and well-being.*

- *Finally, there are those very few people who will sacrifice anything to achieve their goals. These are often the people who become rich or famous or both. No price is too high, and no pain is too great for them to endure if it means achieving the goals they set.*

None of these five groups are right, and none are wrong. They just are. And there's a chance that you lie somewhere across this range; therefore, the question becomes what are you willing to sacrifice to achieve what you want. Because every success comes from sacrifice.

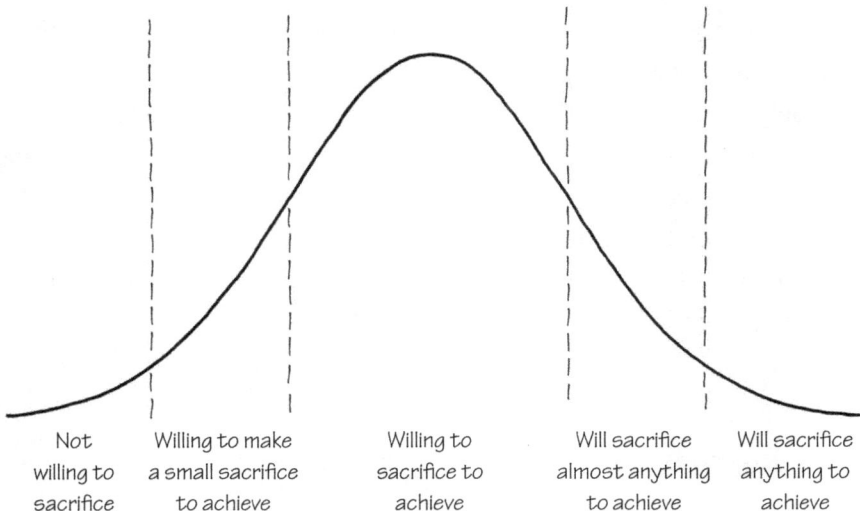

| Not willing to sacrifice | Willing to make a small sacrifice to achieve | Willing to sacrifice to achieve | Will sacrifice almost anything to achieve | Will sacrifice anything to achieve |

Figure 2.1 **People's likelihood to sacrifice to succeed**

Leaders within Owner Led Companies are likely to be highly motivated. They are likely motivated enough to sacrifice more than the average person to achieve what they want. They didn't reach their current level of success without motivation because motivation always pulls you to succeed. If you've got it, motivation is easy.

When you've got motivation, your partner might be telling you to stop working on weekends. Perhaps you're being told to stop talking about work and find a hobby. Maybe your motivation has even cost you dearly.

Thinking back to the attributes of discipline and patience for a leader from chapter one, discipline is hard. Patience is hard. These are both push things, they're not a pull thing like motivation.

Having Jocko Willink tell you that you need the discipline to wake up at 4.30 am will not make a difference if you're not motivated. Equally, having Warren Buffet tell you the virtues of compounding and why you need patience will not matter if you aren't motivated to invest. Discipline and patience are especially hard if you are highly motivated because raw motivation isn't disciplined and it isn't patient. Raw motivation is full-on and it wants to get everything done, any way possible, right now!

But what created motivation for you? Maybe when you were in school, a teacher told you that you would never amount to much, and now you're motivated to prove them wrong. Or maybe you found affection from a parent when you accomplished something and continue to subconsciously seek this.

David McClelland's theory about needs is well-known in understanding motivation. According to this theory, people develop three main types of needs from their life experiences:

- *The need for achievement*

- *The need for affiliation*

- *The need for power*

Each person has their own mix of these needs, and the strongest need usually guides their behaviour.

McClelland's Thematic Apperception Test (TAT) helps us understand what drives people. In this test, people are shown clear pictures and asked to tell a story about them, explaining who the characters are, what they're doing, and why. The idea is that these stories show their thoughts and motivations. For example, if someone talks about success, meeting deadlines, or coming up with new ideas, it may show they have a strong need to achieve. This need to achieve often comes from childhood experiences where their hard work was rewarded, which helps them develop persistence. As adults, people with a strong need to achieve are always trying to do better, constantly improving themselves and setting big goals.

McClelland also studied how motivated different countries were by analysing the themes in their children's stories, particularly around the need for achievement. From this, he developed a rating system called the 'n-factor.' He found that countries with higher n-factor scores tended to experience greater economic prosperity in the following generation. People with a strong need to achieve often thrive in roles where they can work independently and be judged on their own performance. However, they may struggle in management positions, where success depends on motivating others rather than focusing solely on personal achievement.

On the other hand, stories in McClelland's test about spending time with friends or family might show a high need for affiliation. These people want to be accepted and enjoy social interactions and companionship. They find satisfaction in building relationships and being part of a supportive group. They are usually good team members but might not be as effective in leadership roles.

Lastly, stories about trying to influence others or make a big impact may indicate a high need for power. People with this need want to control and influence their surroundings. If not managed well, this desire for power can lead to negative behaviours, like seeking personal gain or prestige at the cost of others' well-being. If you've ever heard someone describe a person working at a corporation as being just a number, it's worth considering that those with a need for power love to accumulate and talk about those numbers.

So people with a need for power might be drawn to corporations that they believe possess power, whereas those with a need for achievement might be drawn to run an Owner Led Company.

These people might look like you, but they are not like you.

While this need for achievement is a useful mechanism for motivation, there are three fundamental problems.

There is no direction.

There is no limit, meaning:

people can sacrifice too much.

And I've lived that. I've paid the bigger price. I've seen friends and clients pay the bigger price. And it breaks my heart that motivated people start businesses full of hope, only to find that entrepreneurship doesn't deliver what it says on the tin. It promises freedom, but too often, it leads to stress, frustration, and burnout instead.

It's deeply saddening to think of the millions of people who have become impulsive risk-takers, driven by a need for achievement, and sacrificed too much.

What's inside and driving you - DNA

Is entrepreneurship nature or nurture?

For me, this question is deeply personal. My mother was an entrepreneur, as was her father, and his father before him. Many of my other relatives have also started businesses. But I didn't meet my mother until I was 24 years old because I was adopted. And by that point, I had already started two businesses.

Growing up in my adopted family, I had never met anyone who owned or ran a business. I'd never even met a supervisor or manager. Yet despite having no mentor, no role model, and definitely no experience, I took the risk and started a business. Twice. It felt like the only real choice for me. Almost as if I were wired for it. Like entrepreneurship was in my DNA.

Back in 2008, researchers Nicos Nicolaou and Shane Scott explored this very idea. Their study, *Is the Tendency to Engage in Entrepreneurship Genetic?*, revealed that genetic factors account for 30 to 40 percent of the variation in entrepreneurial tendencies.

A decade later, in 2018, leading behavioural geneticist Robert Plomin, who has published more than 800 papers on the subject, released his book *The Blueprint*. He argued that genetics have a far greater influence on who we become than previously believed. As he puts it, *'Parents matter, schools matter, and life experiences matter, but they don't make a difference in shaping who we are. DNA is the only thing that makes a substantial systematic difference, accounting for 50 percent of the variance in psychological traits. The rest comes down to chance environmental experiences that do not have long-term effects.'*

Fast forward to 2022, when I set out to improve my health and began working with Paloma Hatami from MyGene in Melbourne. Her program analyses your DNA, bloodwork and family history, then compares the results against thousands of peer-reviewed studies to create a personalised lifespan plan that helps you live the best life possible, for as long as possible, with the genes you have.

As I got to know Paloma, she explained that my lived experience closely reflected what the science says about how DNA can predispose some people to entrepreneurship and leadership. When she showed me how these genetic traits shaped who I was, a lot of my life suddenly made more sense.

Later, when Paloma joined me on my podcast, she shared how the top entrepreneurs she had genotyped all showed high levels of ADHD and hyperfocus. While those traits can drive incredible focus and achievement, they also lead people to ignore important aspects of their lives, experience higher stress, and struggle more often with mental health issues.

Of course, this does not mean that everyone with this genetic recipe becomes an entrepreneur. But it does suggest there is a combination of DNA factors that make entrepreneurship more likely. Whether it is the genetic traits we have discussed or others still being uncovered, some people are simply more predisposed to take big risks, pursue challenging goals, and feel drawn to building something bigger simply because of who they are.

When you combine this genetic predisposition with a high *Need for Achievement*, the internal drive to accomplish big goals, you create people who are not just inclined to build businesses but feel compelled to. And yet, there is still one more factor at play: the influence of the society around you.

What's coming at you from the outside world–the society that's influencing you

We live a world where bigger is revered.

We celebrate the tallest building in the world. We talk endlessly about the biggest sporting event in the biggest sporting stadium. There are countless lists about the world's biggest companies, or the fastest growing companies. Every day newspapers all over the world dedicate miles of print to companies whose share price moved, or have managed to get a little bit bigger.

Vacuous marketing people try to sell you 'growth hacks' as a way to grow your revenues faster. Many people aspire to become famous on the internet with the largest possible audience, often trading all their time, dignity and privacy, but perhaps deep inside, not really knowing why they desire that audience to keep getting bigger.

Gross Domestic Product is the measuring stick for every country's economy, and the fastest-growing country in recorded history is most likely China, recording around 10 per cent GDP growth on average each year for 30 years from around 1978 onward. The modernisation of China, helping those in extreme rural poverty come to cities and enjoy better lives, is one of the world's great success stories. Yet for all that focus on growing GDP, net migration has remained negative for the same period, averaging -0.266 per 1,000 population over the past 20 years.

Over the same period Australia has recorded average GDP growth of 3.29 per cent and a net migration rate of 5.99 per cent. Even worse, Australia is the most popular destination in the world for migrating Chinese High Net Worth Individuals (HNWI) who have more than U.S. $1m to invest, removing sought after wealthy entrepreneurs from the Chinese economy.

China might be bigger, it might be growing faster with more opportunity, but according to population movements, Australia is better.

The mantra of the mainstream media is if it bleeds, it leads. If you turn on the TV news right now, you will most likely be greeted by a horrifying crime or tragedy. The mainstream newspapers write about things that rarely, if ever, happen in people's lives every day on almost every page because their job is to sell advertising. It's the same for the business press. They are writing about things that are so rare and unique that regular readers may view this as normal. Because their job is to sell advertising, if it 'bleeds', it leads. The business media sell outlier stories and glorify extremes. They entertain the audience to sell advertising.

Most of the business media don't write about better events, they write about unique events, mostly at corporations. Open the average business media page and it will offer articles about a legal fight, the earnings discrepancy at a corporation, the impact of a Government change or an acquisition. You won't read how an Owner Led Company improved their gross margin 5 per cent last year, grew revenues by 18 per cent to $34 million and how their employee retention hit an all-time high. Because these are better, they are not outlier stories. Also, they are not stories related to a corporation fuelled by a public relations department. Therefore, the media and authors aren't interested.

When I interviewed Bo Burlingham the former executive editor of *Inc.* magazine for my podcast he said '*I can't tell you the number of people who write about business who have no idea what a profit loss statement, income statement, and a balance sheet or a cashflow statement are.*'

According to Forbes, less than one per cent of the 27 million companies in the United States are publicly traded. Furthermore, among U.S. firms with 500 or more employees, 86.4 per cent are privately held companies. Yet for the news editor who is hungry for regular stories to write about, the constant stream of press releases from publicly traded corporations fills their need, meaning that the easily accessible information about business to write about is from a small niche who are relentlessly trying to become bigger rather than better.

Also, many of the business books on shelves are written about corporations. Almost every business book contains stories about large publicly listed corporations that are easy to learn and write about due to the considerable amount of publicly available information. How many books include stories about Southwest Airlines, General Electric or Facebook? Yet there is also an incentive from those corporations to have books written about them, promoting their business to potential shareholders and customers. Often, the message within these business books is that a corporation or CEO of a corporation did a particular, unique thing that made them bigger, thereby implying that the reader should do it. If Amazon CEO Jeff Bezos does something that's worth writing about, there's little chance that what works for the CEO of that $500 Billion dollar corporation will work for your Owner Led Company. But there is a chance that it might influence you to aspire to be bigger instead of better.

There is a chance that the Jeff Bezos story, or the business book you read, or newspaper article will trigger the mammalian part of your brain which reveres bigger. They are all part of a society bombarding you with information that bigger is better. Society's admiration for bigger things is beyond your control. What you can control is recognising that their narrative may not serve your best interests.

Suppose you have the psychology from life experiences creating a high need for achievement and driving your motivations, and you have an internal drive from your DNA. In that case, it's very easy to be excited by information from our society that showcases bigger rather than better. The pressure from the three areas of psychology, DNA, and society can be unbearable and help us understand why we can easily be described as impulsive risk-takers who are undisciplined and impatient. And often we can't stop ourselves from acting on that pressure, relentlessly sacrificing to our own detriment.

But this powerful mix of forces can be unstoppable when it's focused in the right direction. In fact, it's what has driven many of the greatest achievements in human history.

The problem is, if all that energy is pointed in the wrong direction— if our north star is off and our plan is flawed — we risk wasting some of the most important days of our career. Worse, we could end up paying a high personal price and missing out on the life we truly want.

So how do we harness this powerful combination, make sure we're on the right path, and build the business and life we truly want?

How do we design a business and life that feels full and meaningful, rather than one where we unknowingly pay the price for bigger decisions we didn't think through?

Before we can answer how to take advantage of these opportunities, we also need to pause and consider the forces that are shaping and influencing the business right now.

Drift

When you succumb to the pressure to be bigger, as so many have, you end up enamoured with the next big thing. The next million dollars in revenue. Then next new office. The next new product launch or the next new team member. And it's exciting, and people congratulate you, and your ego loves it. But when you're focused on these bigger things, focused on quantity, you probably aren't focused on quality. You probably don't have the time to focus on better because you're so busy focusing on bigger.

In a business that's in a steady state and isn't really growing, maintaining quality is an ongoing problem. But then throw in a leadership team chasing the undisciplined pursuit of more and you've created a real problem that makes fast growth sometimes thrilling, but often unenjoyable, stressful and draining for everyone.

At the core of the problem is what I call drift, and it's a key reason why we must continually work on the business to make it better rather than only working in the business. The drift problem is that:

- *Teams drift toward toxicity*

- *Customers drift toward indifference*

- *Offerings drift toward mediocrity*

- *Businesses drift toward unprofitability*

Like an untethered, unpowered boat on the ocean, you can't sense drift in a company; you can only see the outcome of drift. Where you end up. And the faster you're growing, the more drift might be affecting you and your business.

Teams Drift Toward Toxicity

If we put a group of random strangers into a team and leave them to their own devices, they won't remain the same. After a while, they might be the same people, but they will form varying relationships. Think about a reality TV show like Survivor or Big Brother. At first, they're pleasant as people get to know one another. After a while, someone says or does something that another person doesn't understand or is upset about. They share that concern with another person, and groups of friends or adversaries begin to form. Before you know it, small tribes have formed, and they're spending more and more time talking about the other tribes. And, of course, what they aren't doing is being efficient, productive or doing high-impact work. This relationship-forming dynamic is human nature, and it helps us understand why there are thousands of books written about how and why you should work on business culture. When the team's health isn't prioritised, drift begins to set in.

Because teams drift toward toxicity, as leaders, we must work to prevent it. To build a better team.

Customers Drift Toward Indifference

If you're focused on becoming bigger, new customers will be necessary. If you're focused on becoming better, existing customers will be critical. So which is more important, the customer you secured six months ago or the new customer you're trying to win today? You might think that the customer secured six months ago needs to be kept happy, but the new customer needs to be won over. If you're focused on bigger, the best people on your team can work to win new customers over, and keeping existing customers happy is, frankly, a little boring and left to others. Over time, customers drift from being won over to being kept happy, and they notice it. Then, like the friend who only calls when they want something, the customers sense your motivations toward new and not existing customers. Before you know it, your business evolves into a transactional relationship with existing customers, and then, customers drift toward indifference.

Because customers drift toward indifference, as leaders we must work to prevent it. To build better customers.

Offerings Drift Toward Mediocrity

When you try to be everything to everyone, you end up being nothing to no one. A leader focused on bigger might decide that the best way to grow is by expanding the offering or expanding the geography. They might think, 'If people buy our printers, they should buy our computers, and if they buy our computers, they should buy our computer repair service, and then they should buy our corporate mobile phone service'. You get the point. Maybe you were pretty good at printers, but the more you try to grow through expanding the offering without improving what you can truly be the best at, the more you're not good, and you're certainly not great at those new offerings. And it's the same for geography. You might be a very good operator in your first location, but if you're motivated to become bigger with lots of locations, those new locations become a little more mediocre than the first. Finally, over time your unique offering becomes a little less unique. One restaurant brings out a new dish that customers love, and two months later, similar dishes start appearing across town, and customers become a little normalised to that unique offering. What was new became normal, and customers came to expect that normality.

Because offerings drift toward mediocrity, as leaders we must work to prevent it. To build a better offering.

Businesses Drift Toward Unprofitability

Over time, it becomes more expensive to operate a business. Costs rise, competition increases, and inefficiencies creep in, all reducing profitability. Consider your business today compared with 3 years ago. Prices on everything from materials to rent to wages have risen all through your expenses column. Also, the competition has probably changed, and they tried to win some of your customers, and there's a good chance they took some. And somehow, there might be more ineffective meetings, compliance burdens, or less productive time. All throughout your business, more and more things are constantly increasing costs and contributing to inefficiency. Then, if you're focused on bigger, focused on the undisciplined pursuit of more, you're creating poor business returns and reinvesting any profit you get into the next idea or fad you come across, accelerating the drift toward unprofitability.

Because businesses drift toward unprofitability, as leaders we must work to prevent it. To build better financials.

A Better Business and Life

When you are focussed on building a bigger business, the painful problems that drift creates arise much faster, much harder and more often.

Because every time you double revenue you break:

- *Systems and processes*

- *Leaders who've hit their ceiling*

- *Cash and business models that don't work any more*

- *Execution systems that lose support*

- *Cultures that become too transactional*

And this is what we've seen across many miserable Owner Led Companies who've come to us for help. Entrepreneurship doesn't deliver what it says on the label. It promises freedom and rarely delivers. But that's because undisciplined, impatient owners, through no fault of their own, end up being impulsive risk takers who focus on bigger and supercharge the drift.

What this leads to is one of the most important questions we can ask ourselves. Once we consider the pressure driving us to be bigger, what are we willing to sacrifice to win the undefined 'game' of being bigger? Or would it be better to control that pressure and channel it toward a better business and life?

So if you want a better business and life, the freedom that entrepreneurship promises, you can't just slow or stop the drift, you must reverse it and compound the results in the opposite direction.

- *You need to compound high-performing teams with soul*

- *You need to compound loyal relationships with customers who refer others*

- *You need to compound offerings that you are the best at*

- *You need to compound disciplined, cash-on-cash returns*

- *You need to curate your better life, by design*

And that is what we will cover in the remainder of this book.

Your better new job

In his bestselling book *The E-Myth*, Michael Gerber told us to 'Work on your business, not in it'. Then Marshall Goldsmith told us, 'What got you here won't get you there' from the book of the same title.

In my book *Made to Thrive*, I outlined the five roles of a CEO: Accountability, Ambassador, Culture, Strategy and Succession Planning. Of course you won't be able to perform those five roles if you are working in your business instead of working on your business. You won't get 'there' if you don't realise that you must do something different than what got you 'here'.

Your job, and in fact, our job, is to take you from being an impulsive risk taker to being a strategic executor. You will need to change your job. You will need to spend less time working in the business and more time working on the business. You will need to spend more time on your own Personal Professional Development, learning how to become better. You will need to spend more time on strategy and more time coaching your team. You will need to build an execution machine and be confidently disciplined about it. Confident because you believe in your strategy and disciplined in its execution.

And then, once we've built your better new job that's building a better business, we can build your better life, by design and achieve what it says on the label of the entrepreneurship tin.

Freedom.

CHAPTER 3

Better Team

'Every problem is a people problem.
Every profit is determined by people.
You've got to figure out hiring.'
CODIE SANCHEZ

The Soulless Corporation

In 1886, the U.S. Supreme Court's decision in *Santa Clara County v. Southern Pacific Railroad* granted corporations the legal status of 'personhood' under the Fourteenth Amendment. Over time, court rulings and academic debates reshaped this decision, changing corporations from state-created entities into 'natural entities' with their own rights under the U.S. Constitution. The Dean of Harvard Law School, Morton Horowitz, later described this shift to viewing the corporation as 'just another rights-bearing person... a fait accompli,' signifying its acceptance as an established fact. In subsequent decades, corporations, now having the legal status and protections of a person under the law, pursued their logical primary goals of efficiency and profit. And in doing so, as these companies grew, the people who made decisions grew further and further apart from the customers who bought the goods and the employees who made the goods. To the decision-makers, these increasingly became just numbers on a chart.

The personal relationships that once built trust and drove success became impossible in corporations spread across many locations with tens of thousands of employees.

At some point in its growth, a company seems to relinquish its soul and transform into one giant system. And then, a corporation is born. Around that time, AT&T Vice President Edward Hall said, 'Mere bigness tended to squeeze out the human understanding, the human sympathy, the human contacts, and the natural human relationships.'

As Hall later mourned in a 1909 address, 'The public does not know us... It has never seen us, never met us, does not know where we live, who we are, what our good qualities are. It simply knows that we are a corporation, and to the general public, a corporation is a thing.'

Perhaps some corporations have engaging, exciting leaders who create energy. Yet the mere fact that the general public viewed the corporation as a thing, as an entity without a soul, necessitated the creation of the first public relations (PR) department a mere three years later. That's when, in

1889, inventor and industrialist George Westinghouse hired two men to manage the company's public image and counteract opposition from Thomas Edison's direct current (DC) advocates. Only eleven years later, the first PR firm was created to help corporations appear as though they had a soul.

While the PR department was established to manage outside relations with the public and media, the absence of soul equally became a real problem inside. And so the first Human Resources (HR) department was established in 1901 at the National Cash Register Company (NCR). For the last 125 years, professionals in these corporate departments have worked tirelessly to convince you that corporations are authentic and have integrity.

Has much changed in 125 years? Today, industries are thriving, libraries of books written, and billions spent trying to make you believe that a corporation has a soul. But it doesn't, and it never will. And that just might be the only enduring competitive advantage for an owner-led company. To embrace its soul.

I truly believe that many good people work inside corporations with good intentions. However, a corporation is really just a system that no one controls. A system that protects itself at all costs. And the system that we call a corporation is not designed for better. It's designed for bigger. Of course, there are exceptions to every rule. Take Southwest Airlines, so famous for its positive culture that the stock ticker is LUV - a cute take on love. Even though it grew larger over time, becoming more corporation-like, I'd offer that Southwest Airlines remained an Owner Led Company, not a corporation, heavily influenced by the co-founder Herb Kelleher, who once said that their vibrant culture was built around the principle of 'caring for people in the totality of their lives'. Not something that most leaders and managers of corporations would say with conviction.

The Problem with Management

It's easy to manage if you work in a corporation. You have tons of support from HR or legal. Systems built into your job and workflow ensure you follow the corporate way. If something happens, there's a process to follow, and you must follow the company line. You're just a number, your boss is just a number, and the people you manage are just a number. Of course, this is terribly soul-crushing for the workers, managers, and leaders, but the corporation doesn't care. It can't. The soulless corporation ensures you follow its system and manage your direct reports like numbers. It doesn't care how you treat them. That's up to you. Just follow the company line.

I once spoke to a friend who mentioned that the following day, she was off to the 'Prison in the Sky.' Intrigued, I asked what she meant. She explained that her workplace, perched in a gleaming high-rise, symbolised everything wrong with their organisation: cold, impersonal and stifling.

Each day, she clocked in, not to contribute meaningfully but to meet quotas, fill spreadsheets, and navigate layers of bureaucracy. Despite the impressive views from her office, the environment felt claustrophobic. Creativity and individuality were discouraged. 'It's like being trapped,' she said. 'You're just a cog in the machine.'

It's not the same in an Owner Led Company. There isn't a complex corporate system to tell managers what to do. There isn't a rule or policy for everything that happens, and you often simply must think for yourself and use common sense. And so, to truly succeed, you need to operate with respect, dignity, integrity, fairness, kindness and generosity. People in Owner Led Companies rarely, if ever, say the phrase 'it's not personal, it's business'.

The problem with management is that a corporation is a system without a soul, and we think that managing within a corporate system is the same as managing within an Owner Led Company. When we learn 'how to do' management from a corporation or someone selling what works in a corporation, we learn to become more corporate-like. We are learning to build a corporation and to deal with people just like a corporation. And corporations are soul-crushing machines for everyone who has a soul. In a corporate system, both employees and leaders dream about escaping. Similarly, the more an Owner Led Company becomes corporate-like, the more the owner dreams of escaping. But you don't need to do it that way in an Owner Led Company.

The more an Owner Led Company focuses on getting bigger, chasing growth for growth's sake and emulating what corporations do, the more they lose little parts of their soul. This is compounded when impulsive risk takers fail to consider that corporations are designed to grow with average people. They're surrounded by 'colour-by-numbers' style systems. A corporation can succeed with average people because the system enables it. Mcdonald's entire business model is designed to take almost any teenager, often in their first job, train them quickly and have them produce exactly the same meal anywhere in the world, and then for those teenagers to leave within a year. The system that works in a bigger corporation doesn't work if an Owner Led Company wants to be bigger but doesn't have the same complex support network.

As one of the Owner Led Company CEOs I work with told me, '*I found that I hired good people in the beginning, but as we chased growth, the quality of the people diluted. So the bigger we got, the more we hired average people, and the more our profits declined.*' Now focused on building a better business rather than a bigger one, this leader is achieving profit margins above 20 percent. These are results the competition, struggling to survive on just 2 to 3 percent, would hardly believe possible.

Ironically, the by-product is that they're now one of the fastest-growing firms in their industry.

This is how leaders of Owner Led Companies accelerate the team drift toward toxicity. Teams will naturally drift toward toxicity, but when trying to hire more and more people simply for the sake of growth and fill roles quickly, the quality of the new hires reduces. Then, the lack of an effective system to control the new hire accelerates the drift. For more on how to effectively onboard new hires, see my books *Onboarded* and *Onboarded for Managers*.

As drift takes hold, the impact extends beyond the team, and it then weighs heavily on the leader. Many entrepreneurs start with a vision of building something great, only to find themselves bogged down in the day-to-day frustrations of team dysfunction.

This ultimately impacts leaders in three ways:

- *Frustration: Leaders hire people to solve problems, but when those hires lack alignment or capability, new problems emerge. Frustration grows as leaders are forced to micromanage or clean up mistakes.*

- *Exhaustion: Instead of focusing on strategy or growth, leaders end up stuck in execution, micromanaging the smallest issues they're paying other people to do.*

- *Disconnection: Over time, the disconnect between a leader's vision and the reality of their team dynamics can sap their passion and motivation. When drift goes unaddressed, the weight can feel insurmountable.*

The Bigger Team Doom Loop

Jim Collins introduced the flywheel concept in *Good to Great* to show how lasting business success builds momentum through steady, consistent effort over time. He describes it through a vivid image of turning a massive, heavy flywheel:

'*Picture a huge, heavy flywheel—a massive metal disk mounted horizontally on an axle, about 30 feet in diameter, 2 feet thick, and weighing about 5,000 pounds. Now imagine that your task is to get the flywheel rotating on the axle as fast and long as possible. Pushing with great effort, you get the flywheel to inch forward, moving almost imperceptibly at first. You keep pushing and, after two or three hours of persistent effort, you get the flywheel to complete one entire turn. You keep pushing, and the flywheel begins to move a bit faster, and with continued great effort, you move it around a second rotation. You keep pushing in a consistent direction. Three turns ... four ... five ... six ... the flywheel builds up speed ... seven ... eight ... you keep pushing ... nine ... ten ... it builds momentum ... eleven ... twelve ... moving faster with each turn ... twenty ... thirty ... fifty ... a hundred.*

Then, at some point—breakthrough! The momentum of the thing kicks in in your favour, hurling the flywheel forward, turn after turn ... whoosh! ... its own heavy weight working for you. You're pushing no harder than during the first rotation, but the flywheel goes faster and faster. Each turn of the flywheel builds upon work done earlier, compounding your investment of effort. A thousand times faster, then ten thousand, then a hundred thousand. The huge heavy disk flies forward with almost unstoppable momentum.'

Collins then contrasts this with the doom loop, where businesses chase quick wins, constantly switching strategies, and reacting impulsively. Instead of sticking with a clear direction, they lurch from one idea to the next, never building real momentum. The result is a downward spiral of inconsistency, frustration, and decline.

The flywheel shows why focus, discipline, and persistence matter. It's not about chasing shortcuts—it's about doing the right things, over and over, until the results become unstoppable. A better team does the right things over and over, and consequentially, the results become unstoppable.

In the pursuit of growth, it's easy to fall into the trap of reacting impulsively and hiring quickly to fill roles. Such a mindset can spark the Bigger Team Doom Loop—a cycle of reactive decisions and impulsive thinking that inevitably results in mediocrity and frustration. Based on Jim Collins' framework, the Bigger Team Doom Loop illustrates how prioritising bigger at the expense of better can spiral a team into dysfunction.

As shown in figure 3.1, the doom loop begins with a rush to fill roles. Under pressure to scale, leaders prioritise speed over quality, hiring B and C players to meet immediate demands. These hires don't have the right skills or cultural fit, so they struggle to contribute. This leads to dysfunctional teams. Collaboration breaks down, trust weakens, and inefficiencies grow as more time is spent fixing issues and problems instead of getting results.

Over time, the organisation's focus shifts from high-impact work to managing low-impact busy work. Leaders, overwhelmed by the growing complexity of a bloated team, find themselves stuck in firefighting mode. The results are predictable: projects falter, morale plummets and customer satisfaction declines. Faced with these poor outcomes, many leaders mistakenly believe the solution lies in growing even bigger—hiring more people, taking on more projects, and compounding the original problem. The answer for the impulsive risk taker is to prioritise speed over quality once again, hiring B and C players to fill roles quickly, spinning the Bigger Team Doom Loop onto its next cycle.

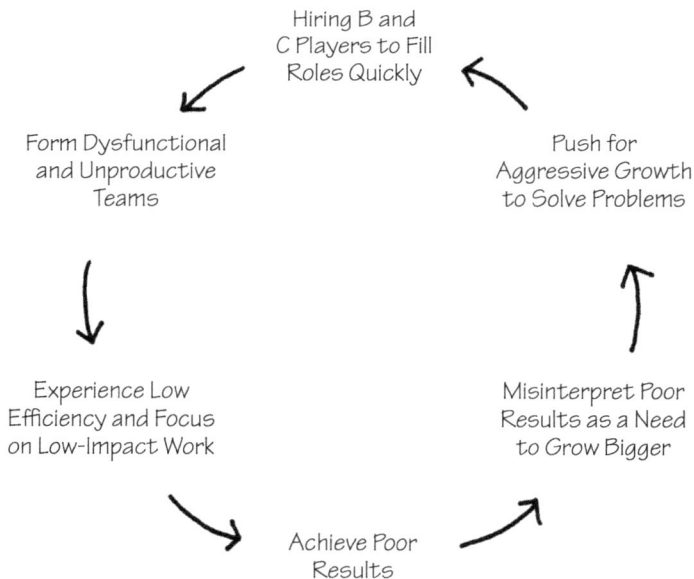

Hiring B and
C Players to Fill
Roles Quickly

Form Dysfunctional
and Unproductive
Teams

Push for
Aggressive Growth
to Solve Problems

Experience Low
Efficiency and Focus
on Low-Impact Work

Misinterpret Poor
Results as a Need
to Grow Bigger

Achieve Poor
Results

Figure 3.1 **The Bigger Team Doom Loop**

This cycle not only accelerates drift within teams but also erodes the company's culture and profitability as the company descends the doom loop. Instead of building a better business, leaders run on a treadmill of reactive growth, where every new hire adds complexity without addressing the core issues. This is the essence of the doom loop. Chasing growth at the expense of quality creates a self-perpetuating cycle of inefficiency and disengagement. Breaking free requires a fundamental shift in mindset—from focusing on bigger to focusing on better.

Ultimately, the owner leader, who was so excited about getting bigger, falls out of love with the business. The frustration, exhaustion and disconnection becomes too much, and they start thinking that selling is the answer. But it's not only the owner leaders who feel this. As you lose the organisation's soul and drift toward toxicity, it becomes easier and easier for people to quit.

Easy to Quit

Why do some employees find it easier to quit than others? It's not just about salary, benefits, or perks. Leigh Branham has the evidence to support that statement in his book *The 7 Hidden Reasons Employees Leave*, based on 20,000 exit surveys. When I asked Leigh about this difference on my podcast The Evolution Partners, he said that for employees, the primary difference between engagement and satisfaction is that an engaged employee feels lucky to be a part of the organisation and, therefore, wants to go the extra mile. Satisfied employees don't.

A players don't just wake up one day and quit out of nowhere, despite what most leaders assume. Too many believe top talent walks out the door because of money or a better title. And sure, for some, that's part of it, but it's rarely the real story. I've seen countless well-meaning leaders sabotage themselves by clinging to this belief, missing the real reasons their best people leave. And here is the kicker, it is usually not about money at all.

More often than not, A players leave because of a bad manager, a disconnect from the company's mission, or having their autonomy stripped away. When those things break down, even the most dedicated employees will start looking for the exit.

The truth is, A players are often willing to trade short-term financial gain for long-term growth and impact. But their patience isn't unlimited. They need three fundamental things to stay engaged: a deep sense of purpose (understanding why their work matters), clear direction (knowing where things are headed), and visible progress (seeing the impact of their contributions).

When an A player quits, instead of thinking about why they are wrong, ask yourself this. Why are they right to quit? Because the genuine answer to that question and the context between the lines of that answer is the real opportunity for you to improve retention and compound team results. It's the opportunity to build a better team.

In writing this, I'm assuming we've all heard of the phrase A players, popularised from Brad Smart's book *Topgrading*, and I like Brad's definition - 'A person who is in the top 10 per cent of available candidates at the pay rate you offer'. If we can recruit those people, then we'd clearly be doing well. Then, if you consider my books about onboarding new hires we can determine whether that new hire is a successful fit, relative to the role scorecard and our organisation. As I researched onboarding and how an effective 90-day onboarding process remarkably impacts retention, the evidence was clear, and I've now presented it hundreds of times. Yet as robust as the Topgrading and Onboarded processes are, something was bugging me. Maybe there's a little more context, a little more nuance. For people who choose to be better instead of bigger, what are the traits in employees that Owner Led Companies could utilise to leverage their natural advantages against corporations in the war for talent? I mean, some A players might love to work in a corporation and be a number. Yet other A players would detest the idea. Why?

More importantly, if I could figure this out, Owner Led Companies can pick the right people to help them build a better company, knowing their natural advantage is that those people would be miserable in a corporation. Then if we build teams of people with those similar traits, we can compound the results. To stop and reverse the Bigger Team Doom Loop and turn it into a flywheel, we didn't just need A players instead of B and C players; we needed people with the traits that would make $1 + 1 = 3$.

If a corporation is designed to grow with average people in average seats and make them think and operate within the system, then how do they operate without the system when rapid decisions are required that need conviction and backing? They struggle. Therefore, the type of person who would struggle in a corporation might thrive in an Owner Led Company. An A player in a corporation might not be an A player in an Owner Led Company.

According to Gallup's 2024 State of the Global Workplace report:

- *23 per cent of employees are engaged*

- *62 per cent of employees are not engaged*

- *15 per cent of employees are actively disengaged*

This means nearly 77 per cent of employees feel disconnected from their work and workplace. Thinking back to Leigh Branham's definition of engagement, it seems that only 23 per cent might feel lucky to be part of their organisation. When we don't have the system of a corporation treating us like a number, we can build a better team.

So what are the similar traits of people who are actively disengaged or would feel miserable being treated as a number? And then why would people be more or less likely to quit in an Owner Led Company? This is what I call The Curious Achievers Matrix.

The Curious Achievers Matrix

If you've ever wondered why corporations spend so much money acquiring smaller innovative companies, it's because corporations suck at innovation. Even though they spend significantly on R&D, and some are better or worse at it, acquisitions satisfy the corporate systems' need for bigger. And even though many of their acquisitions often fail when the entrepreneurial Owner Led Companies are absorbed by the soulless corporate system, corporations keep acquiring. The corporate system is generally not made to innovate or invent in a game-changing manner. It's made to protect itself and get bigger.

Sure, there are stories that 3M invented Post-it® notes or Apple invented the iPhone, but by and large, these are outliers. Many corporations innovate by simply acquiring Owner Led Companies. Even with startups funded by venture capital, the startup community is the innovation hotbed, with founders hoping to get acquired by a corporation and reap the financial rewards. And just like the work we do with Owner Led Companies, taking an impulsive risk taker, and transitioning them to a strategic executor, improving patience and discipline, Venture Capital companies help startup founders become strategic executors.

Why do corporations suck at innovation? A person who is enquiring, curious, and questions the system is stifled in a corporation. The system can't handle it. These individuals find it hard to flourish in environments that value compliance over creativity, leading to disengagement, lacklustre performance, and, eventually, departure.

Yet the enquiring person can thrive in the freedom of an Owner Led Company on one condition. That they are also responsible. The person who is both enquiring and responsible is what I call the curious achiever.

To better understand the way these traits impact team dynamics and retention, consider the Curious Achievers Matrix. This framework evaluates employees along two dimensions:

1   *Enquiring–Measures curiosity, innovation, and the drive to grow. High-enquiring employees actively seek opportunities to improve themselves and contribute to the business.*

2   *Responsible–Measures reliability, accountability, and alignment with company goals. High-responsibility employees are dependable and deliver results consistently.*

These two traits form four quadrants, as shown in figure 3.2:

- *Curious Achievers (More Enquiring, More Responsible): These individuals thrive in challenging, growth-oriented environments. They are engaged, innovative, and highly loyal when their workplace aligns with their internal drive.*

- *Reliable Stewards (Less Enquiring, More Responsible): Dependable and process-driven, these employees excel in structured roles but may lack the curiosity to seek out growth opportunities.*

- *Casual Dreamers (More Enquiring, Less Responsible): Creative but inconsistent, these individuals generate ideas without the follow-through needed to execute them.*

- *Indifferent Observers (Less Enquiring, Less Responsible): Disengaged and unproductive, they are the most likely to leave and contribute little while they remain.*

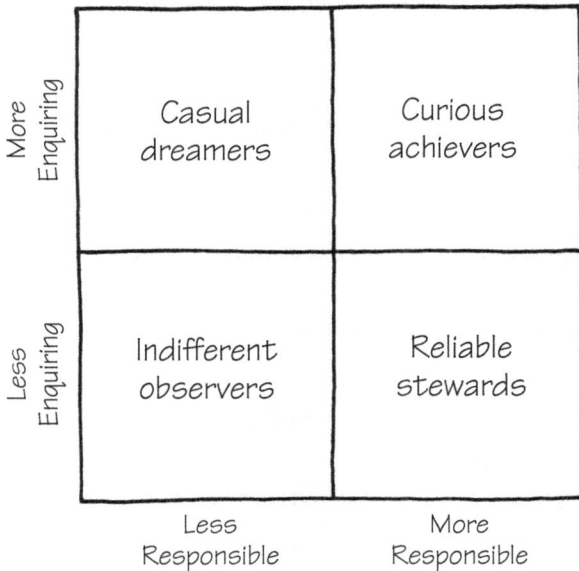

	Less Responsible	More Responsible
More Enquiring	Casual dreamers	Curious achievers
Less Enquiring	Indifferent observers	Reliable stewards

Figure 3.2 **The Curious Achievers matrix**

It's fair to say that very few organisations, either Owner Led Companies or corporations, want casual dreamers or indifferent observers. But I'm certain that you've looked at the framework reflecting on people you've worked with, knowing there are a lot of those out there. But what's really interesting is that the corporation generally wants reliable stewards and doesn't necessarily want curious achievers. The Blank Slate Theory, when applied within a corporation, dictates that anyone and everyone can become engaged and that all people are the same in the corporate system.

In the 17th century, English philosopher John Locke introduced the idea of *tabula rasa*, the belief that every human mind begins as a blank slate, free from innate ideas, with all knowledge acquired through experience. This idea took hold across society, shaping how governments, corporations and institutions think about people and their potential. It created a widespread belief that, given the right environment and training, anyone can become anything.

However, in his 2003 book *The Blank Slate: The Modern Denial of Human Nature*, Steven Pinker argues that this belief is fundamentally flawed. Modern neuroscience shows the human mind isn't a blank canvas at all. People are born with built-in abilities to learn language, estimate numbers, recognise objects, and understand others' thoughts and intentions. And importantly, these abilities vary from person to person due to genetic differences.

Behavioural geneticists have shown that around half of the variation in traits like IQ is determined by biology, reinforcing the observation that intelligent parents are more likely to have intelligent children when raised in similar environments.

In the same way, people are born with innate predispositions and abilities shaped by genetics and further influenced by their environment. Traits like curiosity and responsibility aren't equally present in everyone, and in many cases, they cannot simply be taught. Some people will naturally lack these qualities, regardless of how much training they receive. An employee who lacks curiosity is unlikely to develop it through training. The same is often true for responsibility.

This is an important part of why some employees find it easy to quit. If traits like responsibility and curiosity are missing, engagement and loyalty will also be weaker. Employees who feel fully engaged and see their work as a chance to grow, solve meaningful problems and align with a purpose build a strong connection to their workplace. But employees who view their job as purely transactional, with routine tasks and few growth opportunities, are far more likely to leave, whatever the reason.

Why Curious Achievers can find it hard to quit

For curious achievers, work isn't just a pay cheque; it's a platform for growth and fulfillment. They are naturally enquiring, meaning they thrive when their intellectual curiosity is stimulated. Combine this with their high sense of responsibility, and they become deeply tied to workplaces that offer meaningful challenges, alignment with their values, and opportunities for impact. And when the curious achiever's needs are met, it becomes harder for them to quit. Within the corporate system, this is hard to manufacture; within an Owner Led Company, it becomes possible.

Take the example of an employee who feels they are doing the most exciting work of their career. The satisfaction of solving complex problems and contributing to something greater gives them a strong reason to stay. Their internal curiosity is being fulfilled, and the idea of leaving that environment becomes almost unthinkable.

Reliable stewards, while dependable and important in any organisation, lack this internal curiosity. As a result, they are more likely to view their job as a means to an end. If a better offer comes along—higher pay, better benefits, or more convenience—they may find it easier to quit because they aren't deeply connected to their work.

This highlights the importance of Owner Led Companies creating a workplace where curious achievers can thrive. As shown in figure 3.3, it's not about coercion or retention gimmicks; it's about fostering an environment that naturally satisfies their drive for growth and meaning.

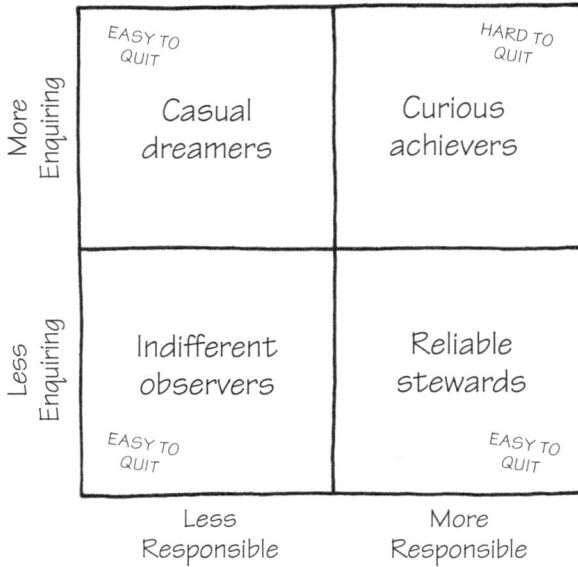

Figure 3.3 **Curious Achievers find it hard to quit**

For Owner-Led Companies, the key then lies in building an environment that curious achievers find hard to leave. This isn't about making it difficult to quit technically; it's about creating a workplace so engaging that leaving feels like an impossible sacrifice. Be under no illusion, this isn't the general benefits of employee retention. Having highly engaged curious achievers leads to a focus on high-impact work and outstanding results. If you're fortunate enough to find yourself with curious achievers in your Owner Led Company, there are four areas to consider if you're going to make it harder for them to quit.

Meaningful Work
Curious achievers need to feel that their work matters. Giving them challenging projects or high-impact roles fuels their drive to grow and contribute. To keep them engaged, they need a steady stream of new problems to solve and opportunities to learn.

Cultural Pride
Pride is a powerful retention tool. As discussed in *Made to Thrive*,
employees must feel proud of their company, team, boss, and
product. This pride creates an emotional connection that ties
them to the organisation. When employees believe in the quality
of what they produce and trust the leadership guiding them, they
are far less likely to leave.

Opportunities for Growth
Provide clear pathways for advancement and skill development.
Curious achievers thrive on progress, and a stagnant role is their
worst nightmare. By offering ongoing learning opportunities
such as stretch assignments, training or mentorship, you can keep
them engaged.

Alignment with Values
Curious achievers are drawn to organisations that share their
values. A strong mission, authentic leadership, and a culture of
care create the alignment they need to feel fully engaged.

As you consider the bigger team doom loop and the advantages that Owner
Led Companies have when attracting and retaining curious achievers, you
can reflect on how to reverse team drift, avoid it being easy to quit and
build a better team.

Building a Better Team

Your team is how things get done. At its simplest, a company is just people
doing stuff.

If you've got the wrong people or they are doing things the wrong way,
you will waste money or fail to capture opportunities.

A better team means that you have the right people doing the right things the right way. To compound your team means building a team that becomes stronger, faster, and more effective over time compared to other teams. In a better team, people are hungry to grow and are regularly evolving into new versions of themselves, taking on new projects and new responsibilities. The team is not compounding in size, it isn't getting bigger, it's compounding in quality. It's getting better.

If you're chasing growth, believing that bigger is better, you can easily sacrifice the quality of new hires for the availability of new hires. Perhaps you start the business with good people, but then one day you hire the available person, rather than waiting for the right person. Then maybe you experience some growth and the pressure is on to hire people, but there aren't many available. So you take what you can get. Before you know it, the small but great team you started with have been replaced with a much larger team who aren't as passionate, dedicated, or aligned with your original vision of building a great business. You then find yourself continually frustrated with the lack of commitment, productivity and alignment to the team goals. You're feeling the company you love is starting to become corporate and soul-crushing.

The Better Team Flywheel

In contrast to the Bigger Team Doom Loop, the Better Team Flywheel offers a roadmap for compounding team quality and results over time. Based on Jim Collins' flywheel concept, this framework highlights the importance of consistent, intentional actions that build momentum and create lasting impact. Here's how the Better Team Flywheel shown in figure 3.4 works:

1   *Hire A Players Infused with Passion*

It starts by hiring curious achiever A Players—those in the top 10 per cent of available talent at your pay rate, who align with your core values and consistently deliver high productivity. These are people who naturally crave growth and responsibility, and who often find little joy working in rigid corporate environments. Spotting their curiosity and sense of ownership early can be the key to unlocking their passion.

2 *Build High-Performing Teams with Soul*

When passion-infused A players who are both enquiring and responsible form a team, they create a strong dynamic. Their curiosity sparks innovation and challenges the norm, while their responsibility ensures things actually get done. By nurturing these qualities, you build an environment where each person can thrive, both individually and together.

3 *Higher Efficiency and Focus on High Impact Work*

When high-performing, values-aligned team members come together, everyday tasks become more efficient, freeing time for the work that truly matters. Because they're enquiring and responsible curious achievers, they channel every bit of saved time and energy into high-impact initiatives. This synergy strengthens decision-making, fuels innovation, and sets the stage for outstanding results.

4 *Achieve Outstanding Results*

When teams concentrate on high-impact work, they quickly exceed expectations. Clear focus and shared accountability sharpen execution, while an enquiring and responsible mindset drives ongoing improvement. As success grows, morale climbs, and each person sees their contribution truly matters. That collective sense of achievement creates a workplace culture that people are eager to join, paving the way for an outstanding reputation.

5 *Enhance Reputation as a Great Place to Work*

When teams deliver outstanding results, they build a culture of success that gets noticed. Wins boost morale and spark positive word-of-mouth, as employees share stories of supportive leadership and meaningful work. This strong reputation naturally attracts top talent, setting the stage for a growing and replenished talent pipeline.

6 *Replenish and Grow the Talent Pipeline*

As your flywheel gains momentum, your talent pool grows and your reputation as a great place to work strengthens, making it easier to attract A players infused with passion.

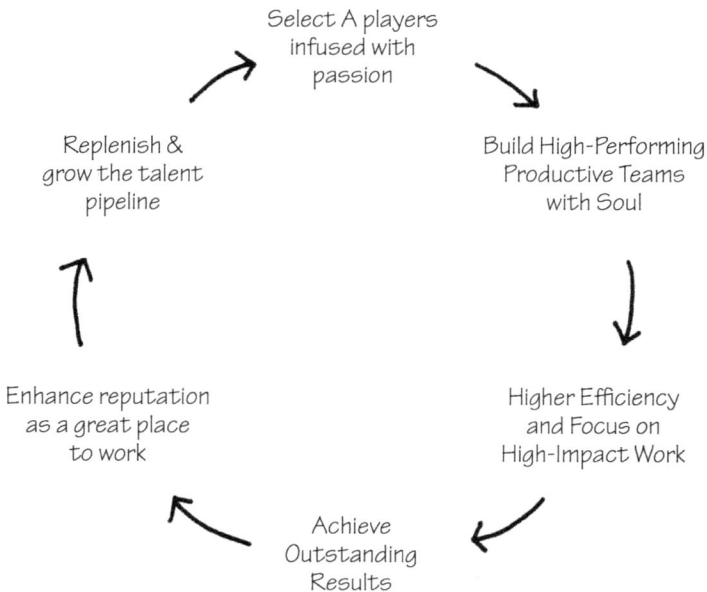

Figure 3.4 **The Better Team Flywheel**

The Better Team Assessment

Building a better team isn't about getting bigger; it is about attracting, developing and retaining the right people who fuel long-term success. Use the five questions below to assess whether your hiring, onboarding, and leadership practices compound or erode team quality. If you can't confidently answer 'yes' with an 8/10 or higher rating, it's a clear signal that improvement is needed to break the Bigger Team Doom Loop and build a high-performance team with soul.

- *Does your hiring process ensure that you consistently recruit A players infused with passion, and would you confidently rate your process at 8/10 or higher?*

- *When hiring, do you actively filter for curious achievers who are both enquiring and responsible to ensure they thrive in an Owner Led Company, and would you rate your process at 8/10 or higher?*

- *Does your onboarding process identify those who are an unsuccessful fit to prevent entering the Bigger Team Doom Loop, and would you rate it at 8/10 or higher?*

- *Do curious achievers feel deeply engaged and find it hard to quit, and would you rate your workplace at 8/10 or higher in this area?*

- *Are you leading a team with soul, where people feel lucky to be a part of the organisation, and would you rate your team culture at 8/10 or higher?*

Building a better team is only one part of the equation. Even with the right people doing the right things in the right way, your success is still shaped by another crucial factor: your customers. Just as the wrong hires can pull your company into the Bigger Team Doom Loop, less-than-ideal customers can drag your business into a cycle of low margins, high frustration and endless firefighting.

In the next chapter, we will explore how to attract and retain Better Customers, those who align with your business, value your work and fuel sustainable, profitable growth.

CHAPTER 4

Better Customers

'Profit is the applause from your customers.'
BO BURLINGHAM

The Transactional Corporation

Jim Wier, the CEO of Snapper lawnmowers, had arrived in Bentonville, Arkansas, to meet with the Walmart vice president responsible for billions of dollars in annual spending. Walmart was eager to dramatically expand the number of high-quality Snapper lawnmowers it had been selling for several years. As Jim explains in the book *The Wal-Mart Effect*:

> 'The meeting started with the vice president of the category saying how it was clear that Lowe's was going to build their outdoor power-equipment business with the Cub Cadet brand and how Home Depot was going to build theirs with John Deere... Wal-Mart wanted to build their outdoor power-equipment business around the Snapper brand. Were we prepared to go large?'

Now, this is the type of meeting that entrepreneurs worldwide dream of. But Jim came to the meeting with a completely different agenda. He came to pull his product from their shelves. While Walmart wanted to scale, Snapper wanted to drop Walmart as a sales channel. As Wier explained to the vice president:

> 'As I look at the three years Snapper has been with you, every year, the price has come down. Every year, the content of the product has gone up. We're at a position where, first, it's still priced where it doesn't meet the needs of your clientele. For Wal-Mart, it's still too high-priced. I think you'd agree with that.
>
> Now, at the price I'm selling to you today, I'm not making any money on it. And if we do what you want next year, I'll lose money. I could do that and not go out of business. But we have this independent-dealer channel. And 80 per cent of our business is over here with them. And I can't put them at a competitive disadvantage. If I do that, I lose everything. So this just isn't a compatible fit.'

For the Walmart vice president, who lives in a world where bigger is better, this would have been confounding. He replied with understandably bigger thinking to try to persuade Jim to scale. He suggested that Snapper find a lower-cost contract manufacturer. He suggested producing a separate, lesser-quality line with the Snapper nameplate just for Walmart.

But Jim stuck with his decision, pulled his product, and lost about 20 per cent of his revenue, focusing on the independent, high-quality dealers. In the process Jim kept the loyalty of his dealer customers. As he notes, '*When we told the dealers that they would no longer find Snapper in Walmart, they were very pleased with that decision. And I think we got most of that business back by winning the hearts of the dealers.*'

Corporations are designed to transact. They are not designed to build long term, loyal relationships with suppliers. In the example above, the Walmart vice president wasn't interested in building a loyal network of partners he could trust. He wanted the best deal possible and would use the purchase volume to get what he wanted. Of course, Jim Wier knew that transacting would only work with a corporation until someone decided otherwise. When a new product manager, vice president, or procurement manager took over, Jim could lose the deal with a pen stroke, regardless of his previous investment or effort. The corporate system focuses on transactions rather than building relationships. It works against trust and loyalty between suppliers and customers. The system transacts.

The Problem with Transacting

It's easy to transact if you work in a corporation. You have tons of support from procurement or legal. There are systems built into your job and workflow that ensure you follow the corporate way. If something happens, there's a process to follow and you must follow the company line. You're just a number, and the people who are your customers and suppliers are just a number. Of course, this is terribly soul-crushing for the workers, suppliers, and customers. No matter how loyal you are to the corporation they will fire you, or stop buying or change the game if the system decides. Because the system doesn't care. It can't. The transacting corporation ensures employees follow its system and manage transactions like numbers. It doesn't care how people are treated. Just follow the company line.

In 1963, Japanese products weren't popular in Australia. The bitterness of World War 2 still lingered across the country, and the thought of owning items made by former enemies was unfathomable for many. Yet in 1963, a Perth businessman called Stan Perron secured a handshake deal with Eiji Toyoda, nephew of Toyota founder Sakichi Toyoda. The deal was for Stan Perron to be the distributor for Toyota vehicles in Western Australia, making him one of the first people in the world to become an independent agent for the brand. Based on a single handshake, that deal was responsible for hundreds of thousands of car sales, even though Toyota had an Australian office and manufacturing plant on the East Coast. And that handshake deal was only first translated into an 'evergreen' legal contract in 2001 and updated in 2011.

How did this happen? These weren't corporations at the time of the deal, but both were essentially Owner Led Companies that resisted the pressure to surrender parts of their soul to the corporate system. Can you imagine how often corporate lawyers have been horrified over the years at the lack of a binding legal contract to force the other side to do what they want? Yet it worked and helped Australia become one of the most successful export markets for Toyota in the following years.

It's different in an Owner Led Company. While corporations often focus on the short-term, Owner Led Companies have the freedom to take a longer view—especially when it comes to customer relationships.

As Peter Drucker said, and as we'll explore further in the *Better Financials* chapter, we must be *impatient for profits and patient for growth*. That mindset is especially important when building customer relationships. We can't afford to waste time and money investing in long-term loyalty if the relationship doesn't become sustainably profitable. Yes, we need to focus on solid profits today, but better customers deliver stronger returns over time.

In contrast, many corporations focus on this quarter's results, this month's contract, or today's transaction. There's little interest in nurturing loyalty. If the price isn't right next time, they expect the customer will simply move on.

But if you're a transactional corporation and you can't genuinely earn loyalty, what do you do? You try to buy it with a loyalty program. Airlines are a classic example. They hand out frequent flyer points to maintain customer behaviour. But over time, these programs often lose value as points become worth less and flights are harder to redeem, and the relationship becomes more about maths than meaning.

Eventually, the loyalty program becomes just another transactional tactic, focused on today's sales rather than the long-term relationship.

The problem with transacting is that corporations rarely build long-term loyalty with customers. The relationship becomes about the next sale—one transaction at a time—rather than the people behind it.

Treating customers transactionally, like corporations do, can work. But it slowly pulls you in the wrong direction. It shifts the culture of your business. Over time, you stop thinking like an Owner Led Company and start behaving more like a corporation, trading connection and trust for volume and velocity.

When we learn how to 'do' customers from a corporation or someone selling what works in one, we're not learning how to build advocates. We're learning how to build a corporation that transacts. A machine. One that doesn't have a soul. We think we're learning how to grow our business, but what we're really learning is how to treat customers like numbers, not people. And over time, that erodes everything that makes an Owner Led Company special.

Corporations often become soul-crushing machines—for both employees and customers. They can't know that customers aren't A/B tests or data points in a survey. They're human beings. And what they really want is to be served by people who genuinely care.

Let's not forget: before corporations came along around 1900, humans spent about 8,000 years doing business based primarily on trust and loyalty.

The more an Owner Led Company chases growth for growth's sake by trying to get bigger by copying what corporations do, the more it chips away at its soul. It is even worse when impulsive risk takers ignore the fact that corporations are designed to grow through transactional relationships.

Corporations are built around legal contracts, not long-term trust. They're not motivated to build future relationships because they don't need to be; they have the volume. Their scale allows them to treat customers as interchangeable, and many do.

But that same approach doesn't work in an Owner Led Company. If you want to grow like a corporation but don't have their volume, you can't afford to treat customers like numbers.

This is how leaders of Owner Led Companies accelerate the customer drift toward indifference. Customers will naturally drift toward indifference, but when trying to target new customers simply for the sake of growth, and grow revenue quickly, the attention given to existing customers begins to fade. Without an effective system in place to manage retention and loyalty, that drift doesn't slow down—it speeds up.

Customer Advocacy and Long Term Value

Imagine you're at a social gathering, and someone starts raving about how delighted they are with their corporate internet provider or the bank they've used for a few years. You'd probably wonder if they'd been smoking something, because it is almost unthinkable that someone would be a genuine advocate for a corporation.

Most people complain about their bank or internet provider, not praise them, unless, of course, the provider is an Owner Led Company. That is a different story.

Now, you might be thinking, 'What about Apple? I'm loyal to them. People even get tattoos of the Apple logo!' And yes, Apple is a corporation. However, companies like Apple are still riding the wave of Steve Jobs' legendary 'reality distortion field,' even 14 years after his death.

Some Owner Led Companies, like Apple under Jobs, can build cultures so soulful and compelling that the benefits last for years. But eventually, the corporate machine takes over. The systems, the processes, and the politics begin to replace the soul.

We have seen it in recent years: Apple Vision Pro goggles, Siri, and Apple Intelligence all launched with great fanfare but never really took off. Apple might still be one of the best examples of building long-term customer advocacy and brand loyalty. But as it becomes more corporate, that advocacy, the magic, is slowly fading.

Trust and loyalty are built through authenticity and genuine relationships. When those relationships are nurtured over time, they can lead to real customer advocacy.

Corporations might be able to build a form of trust, but they often rely on systems to manufacture loyalty. Without authenticity or soul, they cannot create true, lasting advocacy.

Owner Led Companies, on the other hand, can be authentic. They can build trust, nurture loyalty, and earn advocacy in a way that corporations simply cannot replicate.

So think about this: if you are part of a corporate rewards or loyalty program, do you actually trust that company? Are you truly loyal to them, or are you just playing the game for points or perks? Odds are, you are not an advocate in the way we have been talking about.

Let's define what we really mean by trust, loyalty, and advocacy.

The word advocate comes from the courtroom, derived from the Latin *advocare*, meaning 'to add a voice.' To advocate is to speak up in support of a person or cause. An advocate is someone who adds their voice, either by representing another in court or by publicly supporting an action or belief.

But here is the key: you cannot be a true advocate unless you both trust someone and are loyal to them. You can trust someone without being loyal. And you can be loyal without truly trusting them. But to advocate, you need both.

The word *loyal* comes from the Old French *loialte*. In 1897, the Century Dictionary made an important distinction between allegiance and loyalty:

'Allegiance is a matter of principle, and applies especially to conduct; the oath of allegiance covers conduct only. Loyalty is a matter of both principle and sentiment, conduct and feeling; it implies enthusiasm and devotion.'

Trust has even deeper roots—from the Old English word *treowian*, meaning to believe, to be faithful, firm, solid, or steadfast.

So, to create advocacy, both trust and loyalty must be present. But either can exist on its own:

- *A soldier might be loyal to the military, but not trust it. That soldier wouldn't advocate for it, or speak positively on its behalf.*

- *A customer might be loyal to a local shop because of the personal connection or experience, but not fully trust that they'll always stock what they need.*

- *An Amazon customer may trust that they'll get low prices and fast delivery, but if someone else offers something more convenient, they'll jump ship. That's trust without loyalty. And without loyalty, they're not an advocate for Amazon.*

Let me give a personal example.

I'm a member of the Qantas Frequent Flyer program here in Australia. But I'm not telling my friends how great it is, because I'm not an advocate. Over the years, there have been plenty of times they could have done what they promised, but did not.

That is the difference. I trust they can do what they say, but I do not believe they must.

Loyalty means believing someone will act in your best interests, even when it is not easy or convenient. And when I reflect on it, there is not a single loyalty program I am part of that truly impacts my customer loyalty. Not one.

This is the gap most companies miss. They work to manufacture trust, but they fail to earn loyalty. And without both, they can never create true advocacy.

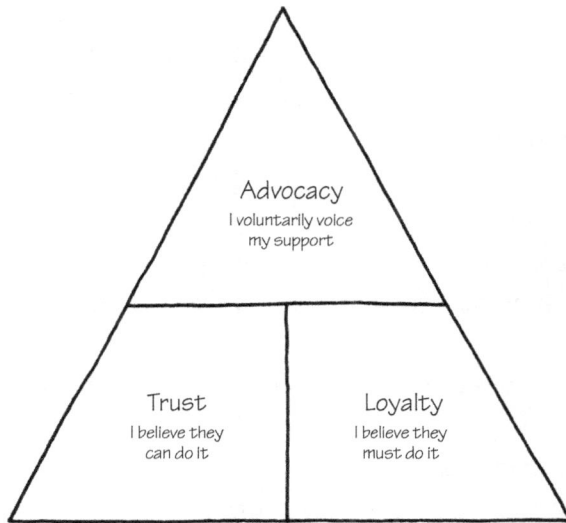

Figure 4.1 **Customer Advocacy Pyramid**

As shown in Figure 4.1, trust, loyalty, and advocacy form a pyramid.

- *With trust, I believe you can do what you say.*

- *With loyalty, I believe you must do it.*

- *And with advocacy, I choose to voice my support.*

Advocacy sits at the top of the pyramid, but it only happens when both trust and loyalty are genuinely earned. Without one, customers may stick around for a while, but they will never actively promote your business. Corporations often struggle with this because they treat relationships as transactions. They try to engineer trust through loyalty programs or marketing campaigns, but without authenticity and real human connection, long-term customer support remains out of reach.

Owner Led Companies have the chance to do things differently. By building trust and earning loyalty through genuine care and meaningful service, they create customers who not only stay but proudly share their experience with others.

When you achieve trust, loyalty and advocacy as an Owner Led Company, you create meaningful differentiation with your customers that sets you apart from corporate competitors. This deeper connection not only makes you different strategically but also unlocks greater long-term value. That is where Lifetime Value (LTV) becomes a powerful lens. LTV helps you measure how much revenue a single customer will generate over the full course of their relationship with your business. To calculate it, use this formula:

$$LTV = Average\ Purchase\ Value \times Purchase\ Frequency \times Average\ Customer\ Lifespan$$

Let us say your average customer spends $2,000 per year, buys once a year, and stays for 3 years. That gives you an LTV of $6,000. But now imagine that through better service, stronger relationships, and exceeding expectations, you extend that relationship to 6 years and increase their spend to $2,500 per year. That LTV jumps to $15,000. That is not a small improvement, it is 2.5 times more value from the same customer. Then imagine that as an average across the customer base. That is the real opportunity in building better customers.

But LTV alone does not tell the whole story. To understand the power of this shift, you also need to look at Customer Acquisition Cost (CAC), which measures how much you spend to win a new customer. The formula is just as simple:

$$CAC = Total\ Marketing\ and\ Sales\ Spend \div Number\ of\ New\ Customers\ Acquired$$

If you spend $250,000 on marketing and sales to acquire 100 new customers, your CAC is $2,500. Now, compare that to the customer examples above. With a $6,000 LTV, you are ahead, but not by much. With a $15,000 LTV, you are in a completely different place. Your CAC stays the same at $2,500, but the return grows dramatically. The more customers you retain and grow, the less pressure you place on your sales and marketing engine.

Of course, not every business has frequent or repeat transactions. If you are in a market with irregular or long-cycle purchases, such as real estate, signage, vehicles, or industrial equipment, LTV might be spread across decades or only realised once. In these cases, the real opportunity is not just in repeat purchases, but in advocacy. When a customer is thrilled with their experience, they return without hesitation when the next purchase arises, and they bring others along. That word-of-mouth effect lowers your CAC without increasing your spend. In a business where you may only sell to a customer once every 10 or 20 years, the better customer is the one who talks.

This is how Owner Led Companies can outperform. While corporations often throw more money at CAC to chase bigger, you can lower CAC and increase returns by focusing on better. With higher LTV, each dollar spent acquiring a new customer goes further. The compounding advantage becomes undeniable, and it all starts by building the kind of business your customers want to stay with.

The Bigger Customers Doom Loop

In the Better Team chapter, we explored Jim Collins' Flywheel versus Doom Loop concept to understand how momentum is built or broken within teams. The same principle applies to customer relationships. When companies prioritise short-term transactional growth over long-term value, they fall into the trap of the Bigger Customers Doom Loop—a cycle that erodes profitability, customer loyalty, and strategic focus.

As shown in Figure 4.2, this doom loop begins with an obsession for top-line growth. Leaders set aggressive targets to acquire more customers, focusing on volume instead of value. But as the business stretches to meet those targets, it shifts from delighting customers to merely satisfying them, meeting expectations but never exceeding them.

Without the time or discipline to nurture deeper connections, the business builds transactional relationships that are shallow, replaceable, and unremarkable. These customers spend less over time, leading to a lower lifetime value (LTV) per customer. Because they do not feel emotionally connected or loyal, they are quick to leave when a competitor offers a better deal.

With low LTV and shallow engagement, profits remain minimal. Margins shrink as CAC rises, forcing the business to invest more just to stand still.

And so the cycle continues. With no real loyalty or advocacy to fuel sustainable growth, the business is forced to chase more and more new customers. This spins the Bigger Customers Doom Loop into its next cycle.

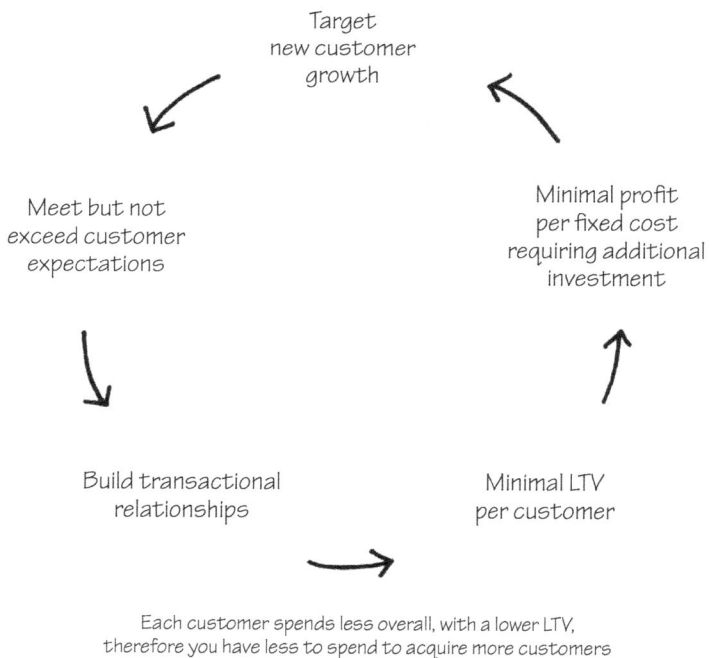

Target
new customer
growth

Meet but not
exceed customer
expectations

Minimal profit
per fixed cost
requiring additional
investment

Build transactional
relationships

Minimal LTV
per customer

Each customer spends less overall, with a lower LTV,
therefore you have less to spend to acquire more customers

Figure 4.2 **Bigger Customers Doom Loop**

Over time, the business shifts from developing customer relationships to managing surface-level transactions. Leaders, overwhelmed by declining margins and rising acquisition costs, find themselves stuck in a constant scramble to find new customers. The outcomes are predictable: loyalty fades, referrals dry up, and profitability suffers. Faced with these issues, many leaders wrongly believe the answer is to grow even bigger. They launch new campaigns, expand into more markets, and throw more money at customer acquisition. For the impulsive risk taker, the instinct is to double down—chasing volume over value and speed over substance—which only accelerates the next painful rotation of the Bigger Customers Doom Loop.

This cycle not only accelerates customer drift toward indifference, but also erodes the business's ability to build long-term customer relationships. As the company continues around the doom loop, leaders find themselves on a treadmill of short-term growth. Leaders fall into a pattern of chasing new customers, launching promotions and cutting margins just to stay afloat. This is the essence of the doom loop. Chasing growth at the expense of loyalty creates a self-perpetuating cycle of transactional engagement and diminishing returns. Breaking free requires a fundamental shift in mindset, from focusing on bigger to focusing on better.

Over time, the owner leader who was once energised by the thrill of winning new customers begins to burn out. The constant churn, margin pressure and relentless pressure from transactional customers take their toll. Exhausted and disillusioned, selling the business starts to feel like the only escape. An Owner Led Company cannot succeed in trying to scale by transacting. They simply do not have the volume of a corporation to absorb the cost of low-margin, low-loyalty relationships. As loyalty fades and trust erodes, the business loses its soul and any real chance of customer advocacy. And when the soul is gone, customers do not just drift away; they disappear without a second thought.

Easy to Substitute

Why do some customers become loyal fans who refer others, return often and act as your unofficial sales force, while others vanish at the first sign of a discount from a competitor? The answer lies not in pricing or convenience but in whether you have earned the right to matter.

Many Owner Led Companies underestimate just how substitutable they've become. They're so busy trying to acquire the next customer that they forget about the last one. But here's the thing: if you don't deliberately build a business that exceeds expectations, you'll default to one that barely meets them.

And when you merely meet expectations, customers become indifferent and you invite substitution.

Genuine advocacy does not come from clever branding or catchy taglines. It comes from delivering such remarkable value that the customer would not dream of going elsewhere. It is what fuels the Better Customers Flywheel: by consistently exceeding expectations, you create advocates who return more often, refer new business, and extend their lifetime value. Their loyalty is no longer transactional. It's emotional.

This is the quiet superpower of an Owner Led Company. You do not need mass-market reach or a corporate marketing machine when your customers are doing your selling for you. But you do need the discipline to resist short-term acquisition tactics and instead invest in the long game, delighting the customers you already have.

The question is not whether your product or service is good enough. The question is: would your customer fight to keep working with you? If the answer is no, you have got work to do. Because in a world where so much is average, exceeding expectations is the way to utilise the natural advantage of an Owner Led Company, improve LTV, and reduce CAC.

The Genuine Advocates Matrix

Some customers will keep buying from you year after year. Others will drift away the moment a cheaper or easier option appears. It is not just about pricing or features. It is about the strength of the relationship, and whether that relationship continues to deepen or slowly fades into indifference.

Too often, impulsive risk takers at Owner Led Companies get caught chasing new business. They focus on winning the next deal, while existing customers are handed off, managed, and maintained. Over time, existing customers notice. What began as a relationship built on trust becomes a routine. The service is fine, but unremarkable. The promises are kept, but not exceeded. Loyalty begins to fade.

But when you consistently go beyond what was promised, when you do what you said you would, without being asked, every time, you create something different.

You create better customers by building something better. Better service, better outcomes, better follow-through. Better customers are not a by-product of marketing. They result from consistently exceeding expectations.

To more deeply understand this, consider the Genuine Advocates Matrix. This framework evaluates customers along two dimensions:

1 *Trust: They believe you'll do what you say you will. You've earned their confidence through consistency and delivery.*

2 *Loyalty: They believe you must do it, because they have emotionally committed to your business. They do not just choose you, they feel they have no choice but to choose you.*

These two traits form four quadrants, as shown in Figure 4.3:

- *Genuine Advocates (High Trust, High Loyalty): These customers believe in your product, your people, and your promise. They do not just come back, they compound. Higher frequency, higher average spend, and stronger retention. They are the epitome of better customers. You get here by consistently exceeding expectations and proving you are the kind of business that must follow through.*

- *Practical Buyers (High Trust, Low Loyalty): They trust you to deliver, but only buy when it makes practical sense. Price, convenience, and availability are their drivers. The relationship is purely functional. They are the first to leave when something cheaper or easier appears.*

- *Committed Sceptics (Low Trust, High Loyalty): These customers keep buying, maybe out of habit, inertia, or lack of alternatives, but they struggle to trust you. While they may stick around longer than expected, their patience has limits.*

- *Transactional Dealers (Low Trust, Low Loyalty): These customers are purely transactional. They are focused on the current deal, and they will be gone the moment someone else offers something marginally better.*

Understanding where your customers fall on this matrix is critical. If most of your customers are practical buyers or transactional dealers, you will constantly be spending to stand still. But when you focus on building better customers, those with trust, loyalty, and advocacy, your efforts begin to compound. You grow by becoming better.

That is the Owner Led Company's edge. You do not need to outspend corporations. You need to outperform them where it matters most, at the moment of truth when trust is proven and loyalty is earned.

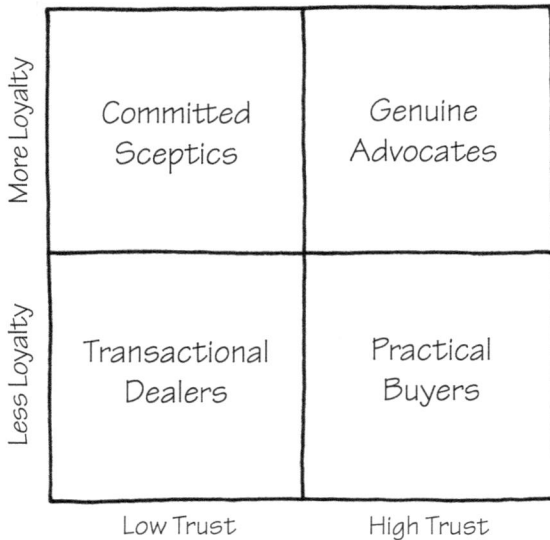

	Low Trust	High Trust
More Loyalty	Committed Sceptics	Genuine Advocates
Less Loyalty	Transactional Dealers	Practical Buyers

Figure 4.3 **The Genuine Advocates Matrix**

Why Genuine Advocates can find it hard to substitute

For genuine advocates, sticking with your business is more than a transaction. It reflects a strong emotional connection built on trust, shared values, consistent delivery, and mutual respect. Their expectations are consistently met and often exceeded. When a customer believes you must deliver on your promise, not just that you can, and you follow through again and again, you create a relationship that is not easily replaced. In an Owner Led Company, this kind of relationship becomes a strategic advantage. And when it is hard for a customer to substitute you, you maximise their lifetime value.

These customers do not just rely on your product or service, they build around it. They view you as a meaningful part of their success. Trust gives them confidence in your consistency. Loyalty gives them a reason not to look elsewhere. The idea of switching feels unnecessary. Even if there is a faster or cheaper option, it does not appeal. Genuine advocates are the customers who align with what you do, believe in how you do it, and would feel like something is missing without you.

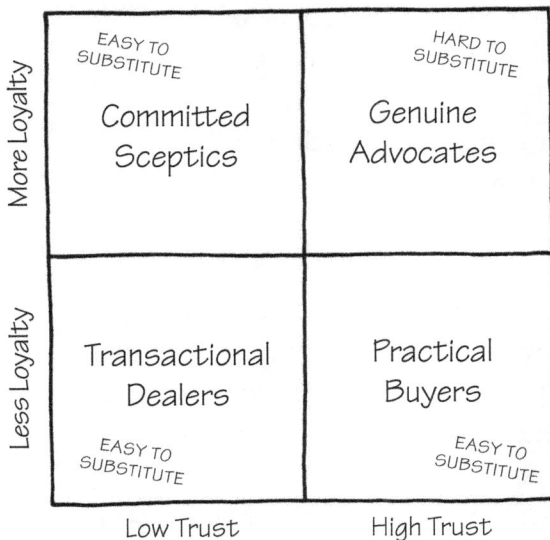

Figure 4.4 **Genuine Advocates find it hard to substitute**

Practical buyers and transactional dealers rarely reach this depth. They engage when it suits them and move on when it does not. The connection is shallow, and the loyalty is fragile. That is why Owner Led Companies should focus on building the kind of customer relationships that lead to genuine advocates. As shown in Figure 4.4, these are the customers who are hard to substitute, those who trust you deeply and feel genuinely loyal. They maximise LTV, minimise CAC, and compound the results of your efforts.

Building Better Customers

Your business does not grow from the sale, it grows from what happens next. Most companies celebrate a new customer and then rush off to chase the next one. But few stop to ask the real questions. Did that customer come back? Did they tell anyone else? Or did they quietly disappear?

You have to find out. You have to find out why people are not buying again. You have to find out why they are not referring their friends. Because if they are not, you are not compounding, you are resetting. Every month becomes a new starting line. If you do not fix it, you will be trapped in a business model that burns through time, cash, and marketing spend just to stay afloat.

This is where so many fall into the trap. They pour money into advertising to push average products with flashy branding. And sure, it works, until it stops. Eventually, that spend stops scaling, and you are stuck with a leaky bucket.

What actually works, what builds true momentum, is doing the work most businesses will not. The work of the 100 little details. The phone call. The packaging. The onboarding. The follow-up. All of it. These things do not just satisfy customers, they turn them into something much more valuable: genuine advocates.

Because here is the truth. Most businesses do not have customers. They have buyers one disappointment away from never coming back. Barely satisfied, easily distracted, and already comparing you to the next cheapest option. They do not hate you, but they do not love you either. That middle ground is where businesses stall. But when you serve customers so well they can't help but return, when you exceed expectations again and again, loyalty builds. Trust grows. Referrals happen. And the entire system begins to compound.

The Better Customers Flywheel is the system that unlocks that compounding. When you do this well, every customer becomes more valuable over time. They stay longer, spend more, and bring others with them. This is how you build a better business, not by chasing the next sale, but by making the last one matter.

In contrast to the Bigger Customers Doom Loop, the Better Customers Flywheel offers a roadmap for compounding customer value and results over time. Based on Jim Collins' flywheel concept, this framework highlights how consistent, intentional actions create momentum and maximise both LTV and CAC efficiency.

Here is how the Better Customers Flywheel shown in Figure 4.5 works:

1 *Focus on Expanding Value for Existing Customers*

   It starts with a shift in mindset from chasing new customers to deepening relationships with the right existing ones—those who can become genuine advocates. You focus on how to make their experience more valuable, useful, and consistent. It's the 100 things your competitors aren't prepared to do. This means listening closely, refining your offering, improving the experience, and identifying the small ways you can add real, lasting value.

2 *Meet and Exceed Customer Expectations*

   When you do the work others will not, the little things that compound into excellence, you begin to consistently exceed expectations. Over time, customers come to believe that you both can deliver and must deliver. It becomes your standard. This is where trust deepens, and transactional interactions shift into something more meaningful and enduring.

But trust alone is not enough. Loyalty must also grow if you want to turn good customers into true advocates.

3   Build Loyal Relationships with Customers Who Refer Others

Some customers may trust you but still leave if something easier or cheaper appears. Others may stay loyal out of habit, even if they do not fully trust you.

True advocacy only happens when both trust and loyalty are present together. Customers who are served well and feel valued do not just return, they talk. These are not one-time purchasers; they are customers who feel connected to your business and want others to experience it too. That emotional commitment makes them far more likely to refer others and far less likely to switch.

4   Increase LTV per Customer

As trust and loyalty grow, customers become more valuable. They stay longer, spend more, return more often and refer others. Over time, this creates a compounding effect. Rather than chasing new business every quarter, you build on a stronger, more profitable and predictable customer base that naturally supports growth.

5   Grow Profit per Fixed Cost to Fuel Reinvestment

When LTV increases but your costs stay the same, everything changes. Your Customer Acquisition Cost (CAC) becomes a smaller part of the equation. You do not need to spend as much to win the next customer, and when you do, it pays off more. With stronger margins, you can reinvest into your people, your product and your experience. With each cycle, the flywheel spins faster and the benefits compound.

Focus on expanding
value for existing
customers

Grow profit
per fixed cost to
fuel reinvestment

Meet and
exceed customer
expectations

Increase LTV
per customer

Build loyal
relationships
with customers
who refer others

Each customer spends more overall, with a higher LTV,
therefore you can reinvest more to acquire more customers

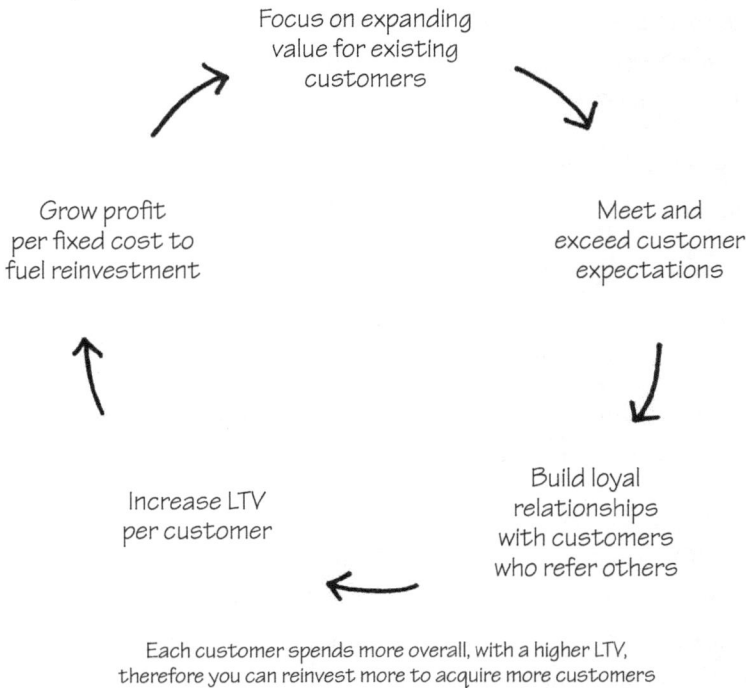

Figure 4.5 **The Better Customers Flywheel**

The Better Customers Assessment

Building better customers is not about acquiring more, it is about deepening trust, loyalty, and advocacy with the customers you already have. These five questions will help you assess whether your customer strategy is compounding long-term value or quietly drifting toward indifference. If you cannot confidently answer 'yes' with an 8 out of 10 or higher, it is a signal that you are leaving value on the table and putting customer loyalty at risk.

- *Are you intentionally improving the experience for existing customers in many small ways that competitors aren't, and would you rate your discipline at 8/10 or higher?*

- *Does your business regularly exceed customer expectations in a way that fosters emotional loyalty, and would you confidently rate this at 8/10 or higher?*

- *Do you understand why customers don't repurchase or refer, and would you rate your process for doing so at 8/10 or higher?*

- *Is your team focused on increasing LTV by deepening customer relationships rather than acquiring more, and would you rate your focus at 8/10 or higher?*

- *Do you consistently deliver on your promises to customers in a way that builds trust, and would you confidently rate this at 8/10 or higher?*

Better customers are only one part of the equation. Even if you earn trust, loyalty and advocacy, your success is still shaped by another critical force: your core offering. Just as customer relationships can drift toward indifference, your products and services can quietly drift toward mediocrity. When that happens, even loyal customers start to lose interest. In the next chapter, we'll explore how to resist that drift and build a Better Offering that earns margin, strengthens your position, and fuels long-term advantage.

CHAPTER 5

Better Offering

'How can you do less but better?'
GREG MCKEOWN

The Competent Corporation

For most of the 20th century, Boeing wasn't just another aerospace company. It was *the* aerospace company. The 747 jumbo jet, affectionately called The Queen of the Skies, redefined global travel. Boeing engineers had the run of the company, and their obsession with safety and innovation made Boeing a byword for reliability. They weren't building planes to please shareholders; they were building planes that changed the world.

The aircraft was not just safer or faster; it was simply better. Better engineered, better supported and better trusted. The offering itself was Boeing's moat. But then, in the pursuit of bigger, Boeing gave up what made its offering great.

In 1997, Boeing acquired its rival McDonnell Douglas. What looked like a smart move on paper, consolidating U.S. aerospace leadership, was in hindsight the beginning of Boeing's cultural collapse. Boeing didn't just acquire McDonnell Douglas's assets; it also took on its corrosive leadership style. Engineers were no longer in charge. MBAs were.

Almost overnight, Boeing transitioned from being a product-driven business to a spreadsheet-driven business. The engineers who once held ultimate veto power over safety and innovation were pushed aside. In their place came managers who didn't know much about aerodynamics—but knew exactly how to game EPS (Earnings Per Share). The MBA mindset took over, focusing on maximising shareholder value, cutting costs and chasing higher returns. And it came at the expense of the offering.

Over the next two decades, Boeing's priorities shifted from aircraft excellence to quarterly earnings. From long-term product development to short-term shareholder returns. The decisions followed the MBA playbook. Outsource engineering. Outsource manufacturing. Slash costs. Buy back shares. Keep Wall Street happy.

And so began the downfall of one of the world's greatest industrial icons.

Boeing cut more than 50,000 jobs and outsourced much of its manufacturing across over 50 countries, dispersing quality control in the name of efficiency. Its flagship 787 Dreamliner was so complex and globally frag-mented that it blew out its R&D budget by $12 billion and took years longer to complete than expected. Yet that was just the prelude.

Then came the 737 MAX.

In a bid to compete with Airbus's new fuel-efficient model, Boeing's leader-ship chose to modify the decades-old 737 design rather than invest the $20 billion required to build a new aircraft from scratch. It was faster, cheaper, and critically it could be 'certified' as an old model, avoiding years of safety testing. This meant pilots wouldn't need new simulator training, which helped airlines save money and accelerated sales.

But there was a catch. The new engines altered the aerodynamics, requiring a software system called MCAS to automatically correct the nose angle mid-flight. In the rush to market, Boeing failed to fully explain MCAS to pilots. It wasn't even included in the manual.

Then came the crashes. Lion Air Flight 610. Ethiopian Airlines Flight 302. 346 lives lost. The MCAS system had pushed the nose of the plane down again and again, until it was too late. The pilots were unaware the system even existed and were helpless.

Boeing's fall from grace was swift and devastating. Trust was shattered. Orders were cancelled. Congressional hearings followed. At the centre of it all was CEO Dennis Muilenburg, a trained aerospace engineer who rose through the ranks and was ultimately unable or unwilling to protect Boeing's engineering-first DNA. By the time he became CEO, the culture had shifted. Financial metrics, speed to market and cost optimisation defined success, not engineering excellence. He was eventually fired, but not before the board granted him a $62 million exit package.

The consequences weren't immediate, but they were inevitable.

In 2024, Boeing's troubles returned to the headlines when the Starliner, a spacecraft developed in partnership with NASA, experienced technical malfunctions including helium leaks and thruster issues, which stranded astronauts Sunita Williams and Barry 'Butch' Wilmore aboard the International Space Station. Originally planned as an eight-day mission, their stay stretched to 286 days before they safely returned to Earth in March 2025. Meanwhile, in January 2025, a door plug on a brand-new 737 MAX literally blew off mid-flight. Thankfully, no lives were lost, but public confidence was badly shaken. Even veteran pilots began checking the aircraft model before boarding. Former Boeing engineers and executives publicly said they would not let their families fly on Boeing aircraft anymore.

This is what happens when corporate MBAs take control. When a company stops developing a better offering. When better is replaced by bigger. When an offering that once inspired global trust is allowed to drift into mediocrity, not because it had to, but because the people in charge believed the offering did not really matter.

To the corporate MBA, all businesses are the same. A plane is no different than a shoe or a soda. Strategy is just numbers. Product is just cost. They believe they can run any business in any industry with the same spreadsheet logic because to them, greatness is optional. Scale is the only strategy. You just need to be competent.

The offering failed. And so did the system that forgot who the offering was for.

The Problem with Competence

It is easy to offer products and services if you work in a corporation. You have product managers, portfolio frameworks, and market validation tools that guide every decision. Systems ensure the offering is aligned, repeatable, and scalable. You do not need to be the best, just good enough to ship. The system rewards what fits the model, not what challenges it. Better gets questioned. Great gets filtered. Over time, more and more products get approved that no one truly cares about, not because they are bad, but because they are safe.

Of course, this is soul-crushing for the people trying to build something meaningful. Only a corporation, a soulless machine, could build an entire business around selling toys that break the same day a child receives them. There is no care, no pride, no conscience. Just profit. They should hang their heads in shame. But the corporation does not care. It cannot. It is built for competence at scale, not excellence with intention. Just follow the company line.

When Steve Jobs returned to Apple in 1996 after selling NeXT, he found a company bloated with complexity and gasping for relevance. Once a beacon of innovation, Apple had drifted. The pursuit of more, more products, more markets, more SKUs, had overwhelmed its ability to be great at anything.

After Steve Jobs was pushed out, John Sculley took over as CEO. Sculley, who had been hired by Jobs from PepsiCo, brought a corporate mindset to Apple. Under his leadership, the company broadened its product range but lost its focus on excellence.

Apple's product line was a mess. More than 70 products and services were in market, none of them performing well, and in 1997 the company posted a staggering loss of over $1 billion. The share price sat at just $0.16. It was no surprise when Michael Dell, CEO of Dell Technologies, was asked what he would do if he ran Apple. His reply: 'What would I do? I would shut it down and give the money back to the shareholders.'

But Jobs did not shut it down. He stopped it.

During a product review meeting, he famously shouted 'Stop!', then sketched a simple 2 x 2 matrix on a whiteboard (Figure 5.1), slashing the entire product range down to just four core offerings: one desktop and one portable model for each of consumer and pro customers. That moment marked the beginning of Apple's return, not just to profitability, but to purpose.

Here is how Jobs reflected on that moment a year later: 'There were 15 product platforms and a zillion variants of each one. I could not even figure this out myself. If we had four great products, that is all we need. And if we only had four, we could put the A-team on every single one of them.'

Jobs' decision was to drop everything and build a better offering. Everyone at Apple, designers, engineers, and marketers, was redirected to focus on making just four exceptional products. The complexity was cut. The noise was silenced. Clarity returned. And with it, the spirit of innovation.

	CONSUMER	PRO
DESKTOP	iMac	Power Macintosh G3
PORTABLE	iBook	Powerbook G3

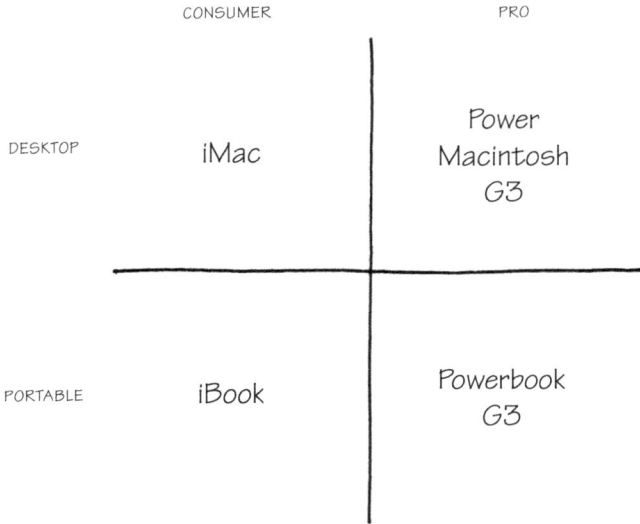

Figure 5.1 **Steve Jobs 2 x 2 Product Matrix**

With that regained focus, Apple stabilised financially and began the slow, deliberate march toward its next iconic products: the iPod, iTunes, and eventually the iPhone. But none of that was possible until the company made a conscious choice: better over bigger. That decision changed everything.

Jobs later described focus this way: 'Focus is about saying no. I am as proud of the things we have not done as the things we have done. Innovation is saying no to 1,000 things.'

The previous leadership had done the opposite. They chased bigger instead of better and created a company that was competent at many things but great at nothing. They followed the corporate playbook: add product breadth, chase markets, and hit quarterly targets.

It worked for a while, but eventually it failed. The result was a company bloated with complexity, shrinking margins, and eroding customer trust. Under Sculley, Apple was competent at 70 products, but they were not the best at any of them. Competence became a cover for mediocrity. A bigger offering, but not a better one.

Jobs changed the game by returning Apple to the mindset of an Owner Led Company. He did not chase a bigger offering. He demanded a better offering.

In an Owner Led Company, the stakes are higher and the safety nets are fewer. There isn't a complex corporate machine designed to churn out endless streams of mediocre offerings. There are no layers of systems built to support constant product expansion, no portfolio committees, stage gates, and no internal marketing engines to make something merely competent appear compelling. In a corporation, the entire system is built for bigger, and it is remarkably good at releasing offerings that are just good enough to scale. But in an Owner Led Company, you do not have that luxury. To truly succeed, you must discover what you can be truly great at, an offering so distinct and valuable that it earns its place not through process, but through purpose.

The problem with competence is that corporations are built to deliver *good enough* at scale. But what works for them does not work the same way in an Owner Led Company. When we copy how corporations create their offerings or take advice from people selling corporate solutions, we unintentionally start thinking like a corporation. Instead of building a better business, we end up creating a smaller version of a corporation, facing the same complexity and diluted purpose but with fewer resources and less room for error.

Corporations are soul-crushing machines for anyone who cares deeply about excellence. In a corporate system, both creators and customers become numb to mediocrity. Similarly, the more an Owner Led Company starts behaving like a corporation, adding products they cannot be the best at and chasing growth through competence, the more the owner feels lost in their own business. But you do not need to build that kind of company. You can choose to focus on what truly matters, creating an offering so valuable and distinct that it stands apart not through size, but through substance. Just be careful, because the temptation to chase more is always there, and that is where many Owner Led Companies lose their way.

The more an Owner Led Company chases more offerings, trying to grow bigger by copying how corporations launch and scale products, the more it erodes the soul of the business. It is even more dangerous when impulsive risk takers ignore the fact that corporations are designed to profit from competent products at scale. They do not need to be better, just good enough in huge numbers. Their systems can absorb mediocrity. But Owner Led Companies cannot. Bigger product lines mean more complexity, and without the corporate machine to prop it all up, the business becomes bloated and brittle. The very scale that makes corporations effective at managing complexity is what overwhelms an Owner Led Company. What sustains them at scale suffocates you when you try to copy it.

This is how leaders of Owner Led Companies accelerate the offering's drift toward mediocrity. Offerings will naturally drift toward mediocrity if left unchecked, but when a leader chases bigger by releasing new products they cannot be great at, or jumping into markets they do not fully understand, the offering often struggles to stand out. It is not better than the competition, it is just another option.

Lacking a clear strategy to define a unique and valuable position in the market, impulsive risk takers rush to launch the next thing instead of honing something that could be truly great. What begins as a push for growth quickly turns into a cluttered mess of me-too offerings. Focus is lost. Quality fades. And the offering, the thing that once made the business special, becomes forgettable.

The Bigger Offering Doom Loop

As we explored in the Better Team and Better Customers chapters, Jim Collins' Flywheel vs. Doom Loop concept helps us understand how momentum is built through discipline or broken by impulse. The same applies to your offering. When an Owner Led Company chases a bigger offering without a clear strategy, expanding good-enough products, entering unfamiliar markets, or saying yes to every new idea, it risks falling into the Bigger Offering Doom Loop. What begins with good intentions quickly erodes focus, adds complexity, and strips away the very thing that made the business worth building.

As shown in Figure 5.2, this doom loop begins when a leader invests in new products, services, or geographies they cannot be the best at. The intention is growth, but without a clear strategy, they do not know where to focus. They follow the corporate playbook: add more, launch more, get bigger. But with no compelling reason for customers to choose you, the offering becomes just one more option in a crowded market.

Execution falters not because the team is not trying, but because the offering lacks any real edge. We cannot help but deliver something forgettable when all we have is competence. Without deep expertise, offerings are launched, but not with confidence or clarity. Problems emerge. Customers sense the mediocrity. It is not distinct, it is not excellent, it is just another option.

The disappointing results soon follow. We thought competence would be enough, but the market tells us otherwise. The new offerings do not gain traction. Customers do not respond, and the excitement we felt during launch turns into confusion and doubt. Leaders grow frustrated. How could something that seemed like such a good idea go so wrong?

As the returns fall short, the financial pressure creeps in. The fixed costs of running the entire business remain, but the new offering, built on competence rather than excellence, fails to pull its weight. We cannot help but feel the drain. Instead of lifting the business, it burdens it. Once again, we find ourselves impatient for growth and patient for profits, the wrong way around.

Rather than pausing to reflect, the impulsive risk taker doubles down. They assume the problem lies with that particular product or market, not with the lack of a clear overall strategy. So they go bigger again, investing in the next offering they cannot be the best at. Another launch. Another idea. Another layer of complexity. And just like that, the Bigger Offering Doom Loop spins into its next cycle.

Invest to sell
more products
that you can't be
the best at

Poor
execution

Response
with bigger
growth plans

Disappointing
results

Profit drops
per fixed cost

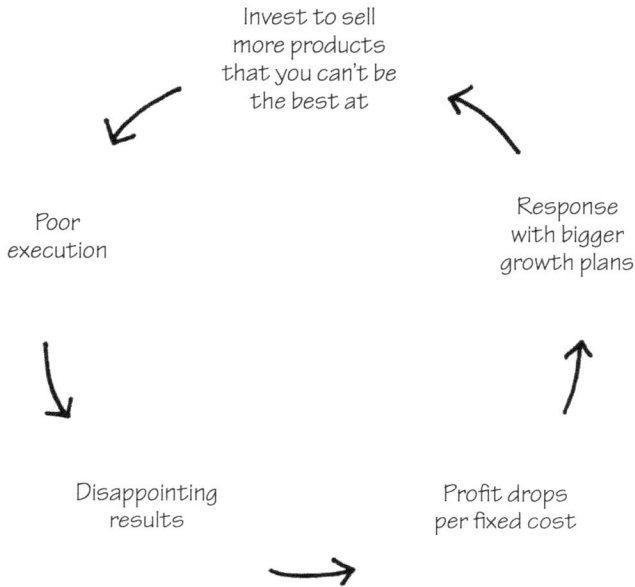

Figure 5.2 **The Bigger Offering Doom Loop**

This cycle accelerates the offering's drift toward mediocrity and weakens the company's belief in its ability to be great. Leaders find themselves trapped on a treadmill of product launches, chasing growth without stopping to ask whether they should. Each new release adds more complexity but less distinction. This is the essence of the doom loop. Chasing growth at the expense of greatness creates a self-perpetuating cycle of clutter, confusion, and compromise. Breaking free demands a fundamental shift in mindset, from focusing on bigger to focusing on better.

Ultimately, the owner leader, once energised by the thrill of a wide variety of offerings, feels the weight of complexity crush their original ambition. The excitement fades. The team is stretched. The customer is underwhelmed. Frustration builds. And before you know it, the mediocrity of the offering translates to a mediocre business that drains your energy, and you start thinking about selling. But it does not have to be that way. Because the real problem is not the size of the product range, it is how easy it is to copy.

Easy to Copy

Why are some offerings easier to copy than others? It's not just about the product itself, it is about how much better it gets over time. When an offering stops improving, it becomes an easy target. Competitors can imitate the surface, because there is no depth beneath it. But when your team is relentlessly focused on refining, enhancing, and building something truly distinctive quarter after quarter, the offering becomes harder to replicate. It is not just a product anymore, it is a moving target, one that is getting better while theirs stays the same.

When your offering is both unique and constantly evolving, you shift from being one of many to becoming one of one. The very act of improving what already works, of sweating the details, fixing the gaps, and deepening the systems, creates a moat. It's not flashy. It's not built in a brainstorm. It's built in the repetition of small improvements that make your value harder to define and harder to imitate. When something is hard to define, it is even harder to steal.

But that only happens when the improvements compound. They cannot compound if they are reactive, inconsistent, or cosmetic. True differentiation is the result of disciplined iteration, quarter after quarter, year after year, until the offering is not just yours, it's better in a way that matters. It serves customers so well and so consistently that they stop looking for alternatives. The more you improve it, the more value it creates. When the value compounds, you do not have to fight for attention because the results speak for themselves.

There is another trap that stops growth before it really starts. Trying to copy the wrong playbook. Impulsive risk takers often mimic corporations, chasing more products, more markets and more offerings. On the surface, it makes sense: 'If we want to grow, we need more to sell.' But without the systems, capital and support structures that corporations rely on, adding more usually means settling for mediocre. You cannot afford to be merely competent at scale. When you spread yourself across things you cannot be great at, you weaken what makes you valuable and make it easier for competitors to copy you.

Impulsive leaders often chase the next big thing, hoping for a breakthrough. They bet on revolutions, quick wins, and headline-grabbing launches instead of steady evolutions.

That is why your most important competition is not the business down the street, it is who you were last quarter. The real opportunity lies in pursuing a unique and valuable position, then evolving the parts of your offering that others cannot see: the systems, the integration, the experience, the cultural nuance that only comes with time and intent. These invisible advantages are what make a great offering harder to copy, not because they are hidden, but because they are earned.

Competence might feel safe, but it is exactly what makes your offering easy to copy. When you are only good enough, you are indistinguishable. And when you are indistinguishable, you are replaceable.

Revolutions rarely last. Evolutions always last.

Great offerings are not built in a single breakthrough. They are forged through thousands of disciplined improvements, layered quarter after quarter, until they become something no one else can match. This is the real path to building something that lasts.

So, how do you build an offering that is both hard to copy and built to last?

If you want to be hard to copy, you need to build what others cannot see and improve it faster than they can catch up. That requires more than a good product. It requires a unique and valuable position, paired with the discipline to keep making it better. It is not just about what your customers experience today but about the direction your offering is heading and how consistently you are improving the parts others overlook.

Because when you stop evolving, even something unique starts to lose its value. But when you keep compounding improvements, your offering becomes harder to match, not because it is hidden, but because it keeps moving beyond reach.

So, how do you know if your offering is genuinely getting better or just getting busier? Let's explore the four places an offering can sit.

The Compounding Differentiation Matrix

If it was easy to build an offering that is truly different, truly better, everyone would do it. But most offerings aren't different. They're just variations of the same thing. Despite their best intentions, many businesses end up blending into the background, not because they lack effort, but because they lack the discipline to evolve in a meaningful direction.

In a world where good enough is everywhere, better is what stands out.

That's what makes compounding differentiation so rare and powerful. It is not a marketing tactic or a product tweak; it is a long-term commitment to getting better over time. Companies that evolve their offering this way do more than launch something unique. They make it more valuable, more connected and harder to replace with every passing quarter. They do not get there by accident. They get there because they chose a path and stuck with it long enough for the compounding to work.

To better understand how offerings become harder to copy over time, consider the Compounding Differentiation Matrix. This framework evaluates offerings along two dimensions:

1 *Uniqueness: Measures how distinctly your offering solves a problem compared to other options in the market. High-uniqueness offerings are deeply aligned to customer needs and delivered in ways that are hard to replicate, through proprietary systems, tailored experiences, or unique outcomes that competitors cannot easily match.*

2 *Evolving: Measures how consistently your offering improves over time. High-evolving offerings do not stay static, they get better every quarter through intentional improvements to systems, service, and execution. The more the offering compounds, the harder it becomes to copy and the more value it delivers to the customer.*

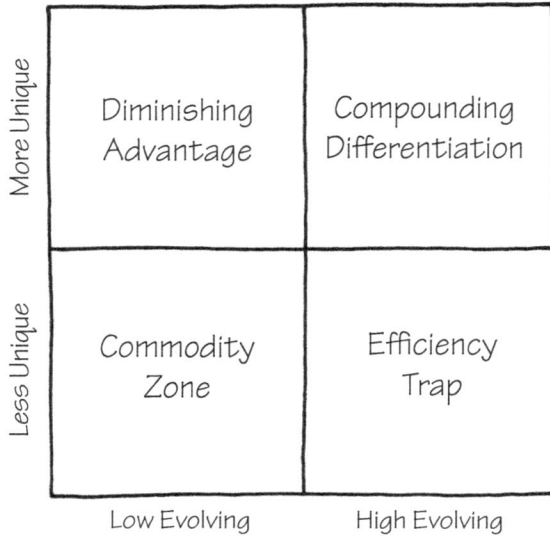

Figure 5.3 **The Compounding Differentiation Matrix**

These two traits form four quadrants, as shown in Figure 5.3:

- *Compounding Differentiation (High Uniqueness, High Evolving): This is where the best offerings live. They are unique in a way that matters and improving in a way that compounds. These businesses are not standing still, they are building layers of competitive advantage over time. Each quarter, their systems, experiences, and outcomes become harder to copy. The result is a product or service that is so distinctive and valuable that it is in a league of its own.*

- *Diminishing Advantage (High Uniqueness, Low Evolving): These offerings start strong, sometimes even brilliant, but they fail to evolve. Over time, what once felt special becomes expected. Without continuous improvement, differentiation fades, not always because competitors catch up, but because the business stops moving forward. Eventually, customers move on and the market stops paying attention.*

- *Efficiency Trap (Low Uniqueness, High Evolving): They are optimising the wrong thing. By making the offering faster or cheaper, but not different, they fall into the trap of thinking they are winning. In reality, they are just getting better at delivering what no one will remember. They are running harder on a treadmill without moving closer to what makes them irreplaceable.*

- *Commodity Zone (Low Uniqueness, Low Evolving): This is the danger zone. Offerings here blur into the background, hard to distinguish, slow to improve, and easily replaced. With no real differentiation, price becomes the only lever left. Once you are competing on price alone, you are already losing.*

Now that you know the four quadrants, the next question is: how do you move in the right direction?

It is not about where you are on the matrix today, it is about where you are heading. The quadrant is not fixed. It is a reflection of your trajectory. Every quarter is an opportunity to move toward compounding differentiation or drift away from it. That is why, in my business, we run quarterly planning workshops with leadership teams to make sure they are evolving in the right direction. Week in, week out, we help firms stay focused on improving the value they deliver, not just the volume they deliver. Because direction matters more than position when it comes to building something better.

Building a better offering does not mean changing what you sell. It means making what you sell better every quarter. Sometimes, that includes dropping things that you cannot make better or be the best at. Whether you are high price or low price, high service or low service, the goal is not to scale mediocrity. It's to compound value. That could mean fewer errors, faster delivery, or smarter inventory. When those improvements become part of your systems, the offering begins to improve from the inside out, not just on the surface.

Meanwhile, your competitors keep doing what they have always done. When customers start to feel the difference, your offering becomes harder to ignore and harder to copy.

That's the power of compounding differentiation. One company evolves the source of value. The other does not. One builds momentum, while the other buys more ads. But as I've often said, advertising is the tax you pay for being unremarkable. Better is the strategy. Better is the advantage. Better is what they cannot replicate.

Most companies do not struggle because they are lazy. They struggle because they are trying to be everything to everyone. Instead of choosing a clear strategic path, they compromise, adding more products, entering more markets, and chasing more customers, all in the hope that 'more' will somehow become 'better.' But it never does. Without a deliberate strategy to add unique value, you end up in the worst place of all: stuck in the middle. As shown in Figure 5.4, when you are not efficient enough to win on cost and not differentiated enough to win on value, you become just another option, easy to compare, easy to copy, and easy to ignore. But choose the right path, and that changes. Compounding value is not just a better strategy, it is the only one that lasts.

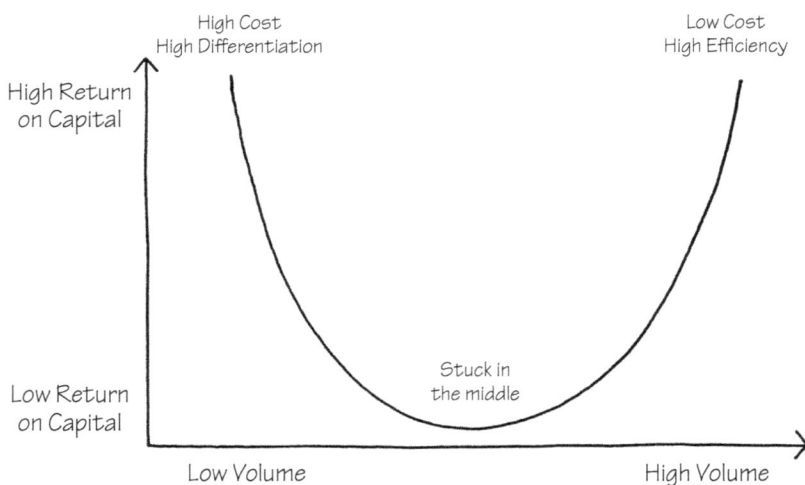

Figure 5.4 **Deciding where to add value**

Why Compounding Differentiation is Hard to Copy

For businesses with compounding differentiation, the advantage is not just what they sell, it is how they keep making it better. Each quarter brings refinements that make the offering more valuable, more integrated, and more irreplaceable. What starts as a good solution evolves into something customers cannot imagine replacing because it works better, fits tighter, and solves more of what matters.

This is the disciplined process illustrated in Figure 5.5. Depth like this doesn't happen by accident. It's built gradually and often invisibly, layer by layer, quarter by quarter, through the systems, standards and culture the team lives every day. And it's this hidden work that makes it so hard for competitors to replicate. They might see the output, but they don't see the discipline behind it. That is what makes it so enduring.

Most companies never reach this level. They fall into the trap of chasing surface-level changes. They update the brand, tweak the pricing or bolt on the next shiny feature, hoping for a breakthrough without fixing what matters underneath. But true differentiation isn't won on the surface. It's earned through the steady, disciplined evolution of what customers cannot easily see but can always feel.

When you build that kind of depth, your offering doesn't just stand out. It compounds, quarter after quarter, becoming harder to copy and harder to ignore.

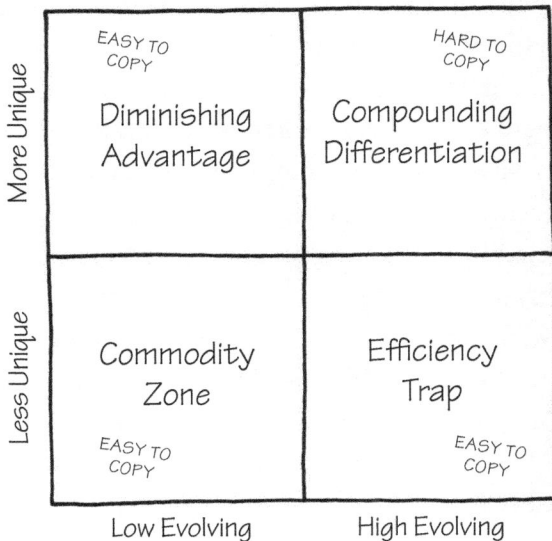

Figure 5.5 **Compounding Differentiation is Hard to Copy**

As you reflect on the Compounding Differentiation Matrix and the traps that make offerings easier to copy, you can begin to see the strategic advantage of choosing a better path. Owner Led Companies that invest in what they can do better than anyone else, and pursue it with relentless focus, unlock a flywheel of value that competitors cannot match. Now, let's explore how to build a better offering that sets that flywheel in motion.

Building a Better Offering

Your offering is what your business is ultimately judged by. It is the value you create and how well you deliver it that determines whether customers stay, leave or tell others. Too often, Owner Led Companies chase growth by adding more 'me-too' products. But every new thing that is not better just makes your offering harder to manage and easier to ignore. A better offering does not come from doing more. It comes from improving what you already do, so that quarter after quarter, it becomes more valuable, more trusted and harder to copy. It's not about getting bigger. It's about getting better.

A better offering is not the result of a brainstorm; it is the outcome of relentless refinement. It is forged in the quiet, demanding work between quarters, in the hard edges of improvement rather than the excitement of invention. That's why Owner Led Companies must resist the temptation to chase more and instead commit to getting better at what matters most. Because when you do, your offering becomes sharper, stronger, and more valuable with every turn of the flywheel. And that momentum, the kind you earn, not buy, is what powers a better business.

In contrast to the Bigger Offering Doom Loop, the Better Offering Flywheel offers a roadmap for compounding value creation over time. Based on Jim Collins' flywheel concept, this framework demonstrates how consistent, focused effort in the right places builds momentum that's hard to stop and even harder to copy. As the flywheel spins, the business becomes more efficient, more differentiated, and more profitable with each rotation.

Here's how the Better Offering Flywheel shown in Figure 5.6 works:

1 *Invest in What You Can Do Better Than Any Other Business*

It starts with a clear choice. Not by adding more products or features, but by focusing on what you do best. When you commit to building around your real point of difference, everything becomes clearer. That clarity spreads across your team and systems, sharpening execution and keeping everyone focused on what matters most.

2 *Execute with Unwavering Focus*

When your strategy is clear, distractions lose their pull. Teams align. Priorities sharpen. Waste fades. Execution becomes crisper and more consistent. And as that focus compounds, you can't help but start seeing real improvement in results.

3 *Results Begin to Improve*

Momentum builds. Customers notice. Margins grow. Complexity drops. The business feels easier, not because the work is lighter, but because everything moves in the same direction. And with results improving, you naturally look for the next opportunity to build on your advantage.

4 *Grow the Offering*

Each improvement builds on the last. You deepen, refine, and enhance your core without adding noise. The offering becomes more useful, more valuable, and more irreplaceable. And when the results keep getting better, you can't help but generate stronger profit from the same cost base.

5 *Grow Profit per Fixed Cost to Fuel Further Investment*

When profits grow but fixed costs stay flat, something powerful happens. You create financial headroom, giving you the flexibility to reinvest in your systems, your experience and your uniqueness, without chasing growth for its own sake.

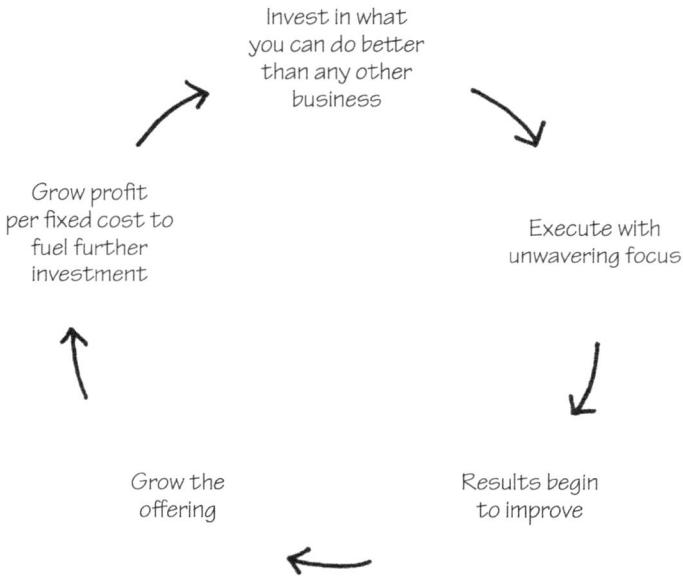

Figure 5.6 **The Better Offering Flywheel**

The Better Offering Assessment

To build a better offering, it's not about simply expanding what you sell; it's about consistently enhancing the value you deliver to customers. Use the five questions below to assess whether your product or service strategy is compounding long-term value, or whether you're slowly drifting toward mediocrity. If you can't confidently answer 'yes' with an 8/10 or higher rating, it's a sign that your offering needs to evolve to break the cycle of stagnation and become harder to copy.

- *Is your offering truly unique, addressing customer problems in ways that competitors struggle to replicate, and would you confidently rate it at 8/10 or higher?*

- *Is your offering evolving consistently, to make it more valuable to your customers, and would you confidently rate your process at 8/10 or higher?*

- *Are you leveraging your company's strengths to focus on what you can be the best at, and would you confidently rate your strategy at 8/10 or higher?*

- *Does your offering meet your customers' needs more effectively than your competitors', and would you confidently rate this at 8/10 or higher?*

- *Are you deepening your offering's value over time rather than just adding features, and would you confidently rate this at 8/10 or higher?*

Building a better offering is not just about creating something great, it's about creating a unique and valuable position in the market. That happens through deliberate, ongoing improvements that make your product more useful, more valuable and harder to replace with every iteration. As each improvement builds on the last, momentum grows, driving your business forward. Over time, this creates a powerful flywheel effect that strengthens your position and keeps customers coming back.

However, as your offering gains traction, it is important to recognise the hidden risks that can undermine success. Over time, the costs of doing business rise, competition intensifies and inefficiencies creep in, all of which can quietly erode profitability. As your business grows, so do expenses, and without careful attention, those costs can outweigh your gains. In the next chapter, we will explore how to build stronger financials, helping you avoid the drift toward unprofitability and ensuring you continue to operate from a position of financial strength and clarity.

CHAPTER 6

Better Financials

*'A large income is the best recipe
for happiness I ever heard of.'*
JANE AUSTEN

The Bigger, But Not Better Media Company

In 1963, The Washington Post Company was a prominent newspaper, with US$84 million a year in revenue and a widely recognised reputation in Washington, D.C., a city where influence mattered. By all outward measures, it was a success. But beneath the surface, the business had begun to drift. It had grown bigger, but not better.

Then its publisher, Katharine Graham's husband, died suddenly. With no formal leadership experience and no plans to take the reins herself, she was thrust into the role of CEO. The company was entering one of the most turbulent decades in the history of American media, and she was expected to hold it together. The team she inherited was disengaged and fragmented. Confidence had eroded. What once had soul was becoming stale, a place where people complied more than they committed. It was a drift toward toxicity, not explosive but corrosive, where people kept their heads down and played it safe.

The Post's customers, its readers and advertisers, were becoming transactional. Journalism was turning into entertainment. Loyalty faded and trust weakened. And in trying to appeal to everyone, the Post began to stand for less. It had become easy to substitute, one paper among many, not a publication people would fight to keep. The product followed suit. In a race to stay relevant, the Post expanded its scope but lost its edge. More sections, more stories, but less purpose. It had become competent, not compelling. The offering was no longer a differentiator, just a delivery mechanism.

The industry itself was falling into chaos. The Post was inching toward the same fate. Across the media landscape, companies were stumbling into the Bigger Financials Doom Loop. They made undisciplined bets to grow, failed to manage them, and panicked when returns did not materialise. Desperate, they latched onto fads and spun the wheel again. Bigger budgets. New formats. Shiny distractions.

Katharine Graham stopped the drift and built the discipline that made The Post matter.

Better Team
She built a team with soul. Her decision to appoint Ben Bradlee as executive editor was a decision to lead with conviction. Bradlee assembled a newsroom that didn't chase headlines, they chased truth. The team re-engaged. They started caring deeply. When the Post stood almost alone in publishing the Pentagon Papers, and again during Watergate, it was that team, trusted, aligned, and united, that carried the weight. That team didn't just report the news, they restored the Post's moral authority.

Better Customers
She didn't try to please everyone. Graham made decisions that narrowed the Post's appeal, and strengthened it. By telling difficult stories and resisting sensationalism, she attracted readers who believed in the Post's mission. Readers who stayed longer, subscribed consistently, and told others. She increased LTV by delivering uncommon value. And by resisting the broad, shallow growth of her peers, she reduced CAC by turning readers into advocates. The Post became trusted not because it said what people wanted to hear, but because it stood for what needed to be said.

Better Offering
She refined the product to be hard to copy. While others leaned into sensationalism, brevity, or cost-cutting, the Post leaned into integrity. She funded investigative journalism when it was risky. She protected the craft when others commoditised it. What emerged wasn't just a newspaper. It was a promise to serve the public interest, no matter the cost. The result was an offering that became not just relevant but respected.

And then she did what few leaders do.

She translated all of that—team, customers and offering—into better financials.

While others chased headlines and earnings calls, she built the kind of financial strength that doesn't demand attention, but endures. She resisted pressure to issue dividends too early. She avoided diluting ownership through unnecessary capital raises. She passed on attention-grabbing acquisitions. She didn't react, she allocated. Into journalism. Into people. Into decisions that wouldn't pay off in quarters, but in decades.

Over the next three decades, she turned The Washington Post from a drifting institution into one of the most respected and resilient media companies in the world. When she stepped down as CEO in 1991, the company had grown its revenue from $84 million to $1.4 billion. It had outlasted competitors, outperformed expectations, and outgrown the chaos, not through explosive growth, but through compounding discipline.

As Bradlee once said, 'We stand by the story.' But the truth is, Graham stood by something even bigger: a belief that strength comes not from chasing more, but from building better.

And the financial results followed, not through force, but through focus. Just as they always do when you choose better over bigger.

The Problem with Money

It's easy to spend if you work in a corporation. The guidelines are clear. Budgets are set. Approval processes are defined. As long as the numbers match the policy and the form is filled out, the money moves. You're not rewarded for asking if it's wise, just whether it's within scope. In fact, not spending the budget can look worse than wasting it. Capital gets deployed on time, but not necessarily in the right place. And if it doesn't work, just reforecast. Try again. Just follow the company line.

It is easy to spend if you run an owner-led company too, but for different reasons. There are no policies. No layers of approval. And rarely a CFO to push back. The freedom is total, and that is the danger. Every new idea gets airtime. Every opportunity feels urgent. You can spend money without explaining it to anyone. But instead of eating into a budget, you are eating into your profit. And when the profit is gone, there is nothing left for your lifestyle. Nothing to build wealth outside the business. You are the boss, but if you are not disciplined, you are also the risk.

That is why financial discipline isn't optional. It is the bridge to freedom. It's what separates freedom from fragility. The truth is, most owners do not fail because their business is broken. They fail because the money runs out. Profitable businesses go bankrupt every day. The better mindset recognises that once you have built a better team, increased the value of your best customers and created a better offering, you must apply financial discipline to protect profits and turn them into lasting wealth and freedom. That's how you move from Cash Poor Entrepreneur to Working Rich to Strategic Investor, not in one big exit, but in a thousand small decisions. The moment you get that right, the business stops owning you. You start owning your future. Then you can build a better life, by design.

What the Silicon Valley investor Paul Graham calls founder mode looks a lot like what we call Owner Led. It works because the person making the decisions is the same person who lives with the consequences. They care more. They move faster. When an Owner Led business is built better, with the right team, the right customers, and the right offering, it can also produce dramatically better returns. In fact, a recent analysis of Fortune 500 companies shows that the few still led by their founders delivered median returns of 1,129 per cent, nearly 20 times more than the rest. They did not just beat the market; they beat their own sectors by more than 6x. Bigger isn't better. But better, when you stay committed and lead with discipline, has the power to be extraordinary.

But to unlock those extraordinary returns, owners must rethink their view of financial freedom. Most begin with a clear goal to get rich and escape the grind, but somewhere along the way, money becomes the ultimate goal instead of a means to achieve freedom.

When money becomes the goal, thinking narrows. Owners focus on quick wins, spend to support their lifestyle and chase growth without a plan for lasting returns. Warren Buffett approached money differently. He treated it as a compounding resource, a tool to acquire assets, reinvest profits and build momentum that grows stronger over time. As Buffett famously said, 'Life is like a snowball. All you need is wet snow and a really long hill.' That is investor thinking. The better mindset doesn't ask, 'How do I spend this?' It asks, 'How do I multiply this?' Until that shift happens, owners remain stuck in the Working Rich trap, earning well but spending fast, always near wealth but never free from the business. That is the real problem with money.

Owner Led Companies often misunderstand the role of money and mismanage its flow. In a corporation, capital is protected by process. Budgets are enforced, investments are debated and spending requires permission. The system manages money with policies and controls, not instinct. But in an owner-led company, that structure does not exist. The freedom is total, and that is the danger. Without financial guardrails, money flows toward what feels most exciting, not what creates the greatest value. Decisions are made without clear criteria or measures of success. Profits quietly disappear, and financial pressure starts to feel like a constant weight on the owner's shoulders. As Clayton Christensen warned, *"Be patient for growth, and impatient for profit."* Yet impulsive risk takers reverse that logic, chasing growth urgently and assuming profit will sort itself out. It rarely does.

This is how impulsive risk takers accelerate the drift toward unprofitability. Every new idea looks like momentum. Every reinvestment feels like progress. But without discipline, money slips away. The business funds too many initiatives, too fast, with no clear path to return. Owners end up cash poor in a company that looks successful from the outside but cannot support their lifestyle or build wealth beyond the business.

What starts as financial freedom quickly becomes a fragile situation. Without discipline, the business becomes vulnerable, with money flowing out faster than it comes in. Owners stop managing money with intention and start reacting to its absence. Instead of money creating a better life, it becomes the very thing that holds them back.

Growth without profit isn't strategy. It's drift.

The Bigger Financials Doom Loop

In the Better Team, Better Customers, and Better Offering chapters, we explored Jim Collins' Flywheel vs. Doom Loop concept to understand how momentum is built or broken within an Owner Led Company. The same principle applies to financials. When an owner chases growth without discipline, spending freely, investing reactively, or stretching resources without clear rules, they risk falling into the Bigger Financials Doom Loop. What begins as a desire to grow can spiral into a cycle of poor returns, increased risk and mounting stress. Instead of building wealth, the business becomes a burden.

As shown in Figure 6.1, the Bigger Financials Doom Loop begins with an undisciplined investment to grow bigger. It usually starts with ambition, chasing a new opportunity, adding a product line or entering a new region. It feels exciting and full of potential. There's no board to convince and no investor to slow things down. The owner says yes, stretching the business to chase scale, hoping profit will follow. But the lack of discipline does not end with the investment; it begins there. Without structured decision-making, there is no discipline in execution. The owner sets no clear criteria to assess returns, so there are no criteria to track them. Budgets become vague and costs spiral without scrutiny. The initiative drifts, pulling people, focus and resources along with it. Everyone works harder, but few can explain what is actually working. Instead of pulling back, the business bends under the weight of the investment, no matter how weak the signals become.

The cracks begin to show. That one undisciplined investment, whether it is a new product, region or hire made without clear criteria, starts to drain more than it delivers. At first, it appears full of potential, but without structured oversight, inefficiencies grow. Sales might rise slightly, but costs increase unchecked. Budgets are exceeded without accountability. Instead of fueling growth, the initiative creates unnecessary complications, inflates overheads and weakens the focus needed for strong execution.

The business starts to feel stretched, with resources scattered across multiple underperforming initiatives. What began as an opportunity becomes a source of rising costs, reduced margins and complexity that is difficult to unwind.

As the poor results become undeniable, owners quietly move on from the original investment. It's no longer talked about. But instead of pausing to understand what went wrong, owners look outward. They look to blame external forces: the market, the economy, the team. They tell themselves it was just bad luck or poor timing. Of course, beneath the surface, it wasn't misfortune, it was a failure of discipline in both the decision and execution. Without that realisation, the lessons are lost, and the cycle is primed to repeat.

With the original idea quietly abandoned, owners immediately start searching for the next fix. There is no pause to ask why the last plan failed, only a rush toward the next opportunity. Something new. Something exciting. Something that feels like it just might work this time. It becomes a fresh spark of hope, a distraction disguised as progress, and a chance to move on without dealing with what really went wrong.

But nothing has changed. There is still no discipline, no clear investment criteria. The same faulty thinking that led to the first mistake now drives the second. The business is not broken, but the thinking behind each decision still is. And until that changes, the stress, the pressure and the drift will keep coming back. And so, rather than confronting the lack of financial discipline that caused the poor returns, the impulsive risk taker shifts focus. They assume the failure was bad luck, not a broken process. So they chase the next opportunity. Another shiny idea. Another ambitious move. Another bet without a plan. Then the money goes out again, unrestrained, unexamined, undisciplined.

And just like that, the Bigger Financials Doom Loop begins its next rotation.

Undisciplined
investment to
grow bigger

Undisciplined
management of business
and new investments

New idea, fad
or direction

Generate poor
business returns

Reaction without
understanding

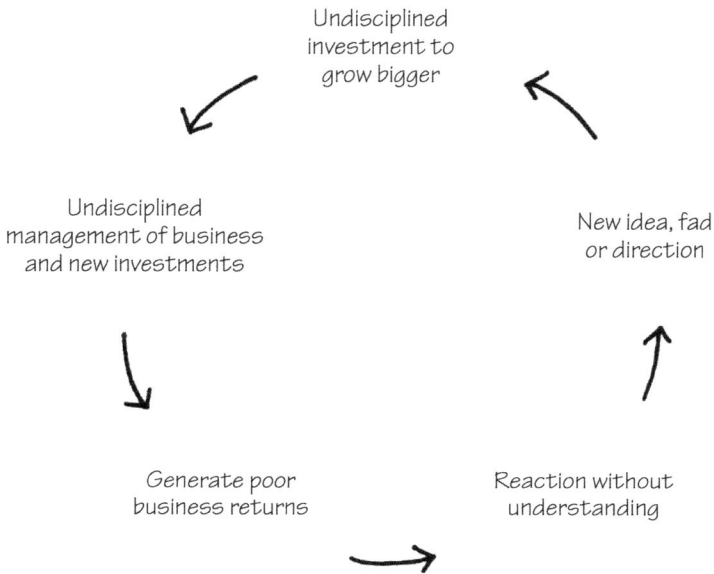

Figure 6.1 **The Bigger Financials Doom Loop**

This cycle not only accelerates the overall financial drift toward unprofita-bility, but also erodes the business's ability to make sound decisions about capital. Leaders find themselves stuck in a pattern, investing reactively, chasing scale, and losing track of return. Every dollar out feels like progress, but the results tell a different story. A story of growth without profit. Movement without momentum. This is the essence of the doom loop. Chasing top-line growth at the expense of financial strength creates a self-perpetuating cycle of pressure, fragility, and stress. Breaking free starts with a simple but powerful choice: stop chasing bigger and start building better.

Ultimately, the owner leader, once energised by the ambition to grow, finds themselves shouldering more risk, with less reward. The business is moving, but it's not moving in the right direction. Cash is tight, stress is high, and the numbers don't add up. They look at their financials and wonder how things got so far off track. But it doesn't have to be that way. Because the real problem isn't how much you invest, it's how easy it is to spend.

Easy to Spend

Why do some leaders feel like they are always spending but never really getting ahead? The problem is not how much they invest; it is how they think about money. Without a clear purpose, every dollar becomes a reaction to the moment rather than a step toward something better.

Treat money as the ultimate goal and the focus shifts to getting bigger, not better. Treat it as a resource and the focus becomes building lasting value. But building value takes more than good intentions; it requires clear rules and the discipline to follow them. Without that, money flows out faster than it comes back. That is how financial drift begins to take hold because without a system to manage money, the business will always find new ways to spend more.

Everything changes when you start treating money as a resource and managing it with discipline. You stop chasing growth for its own sake and start compounding value deliberately. You're no longer gambling on the next big thing; you're backing the few things that matter most and doing them properly. Then profit isn't something you hope for, it happens by design. Cash is protected, investment is intentional, and the business becomes easier to manage, not harder. You're not working just to fund more activity; you're creating a business that funds your goals. One good decision builds on the last, and momentum starts to compound. That's when the business gets stronger and you do too.

Not every financial misstep is reckless. Sometimes, it's a mindset problem: treating money as the goal instead of the resource. Other times, it's a discipline problem: spending without rules, structure, or return. That's how drift sets in. Some owners stay stuck in busyness. Others stretch themselves thin chasing growth. But a few channel their energy with intent. They build better financials: ones that create momentum instead of chaos, and wealth instead of worry. Building better financials and a better life, by design starts with knowing where you stand today.

The Strategic Investor Matrix

If building wealth from your business feels harder than it should, you're not alone. Many Owner Led Companies produce strong revenue, even healthy profits, but the owners still feel stuck. They're growing, but it never quite feels like progress.

Why? Because how money is used inside the business often has little to do with creating long-term value. Some owners keep reinvesting without seeing real returns. Others hold onto cash without a clear strategy. Many stay busy chasing activity, mistaking it for progress, or confuse a high income with lasting wealth.

But real wealth is not an accident. It is built with intention, by design.

The Strategic Investor Matrix helps uncover the hidden patterns behind financial progress, showing how some owners stay trapped on the treadmill, while others quietly compound strength, resilience, and freedom. Not just for the business, but for themselves.

In *Made to Thrive*, I wrote that 'all decisions on new opportunities, new staff or new investments should be evaluated against a documented set of criteria.' That principle matters even more here. Because in an Owner Led Company, undisciplined money doesn't build wealth. It leads to drift. It is not how much you invest, but how you invest that shapes your future. The best Owner Led Companies do not bet on gut feel. They apply clear, consistent rules that guide capital toward outcomes that compound over time, not costs that quietly expand.

That is what makes Strategic Investors, running an Owner Led Company, so distinct and so effective. They do not rely on luck or instinct. They use structure and intention to make capital work harder, building not just a profitable business but a more stable and scalable one. Every financial decision compounds. Every reinvestment moves them forward. They're building a business that funds its own growth, supports the lifestyle they want and creates external assets that build lasting wealth. Their financial decisions are intentional, their investments are focused and every choice moves them closer to both freedom and security.

To better understand how financial decisions shape both freedom and wealth for owners, consider the Strategic Investor Matrix. This framework evaluates financial behaviour along two dimensions:

1   *The horizontal axis reflects an owner's financial discipline. Those with low discipline operate without structure. They're following instinct, allocating reactively, and chasing opportunities without a clear plan. Those with high discipline apply intentional rules to how profit is retained, allocated, or reinvested.*

2   *The vertical axis reflects an owner's mindset about money. When money becomes the goal, it turns into a scoreboard, a constant measure of success, freedom or lifestyle. But this mindset creates pressure to grow for the wrong reasons.*

Shift the perspective, and money becomes something else entirely. It becomes a tool, a resource you can put to work, a seed you plant to grow future returns. Instead of spending for reward, you start using each dollar as a worker, earning more with every cycle. Your job is not to spend $100; it is to turn $100 into $120, then $120 into $144, again and again. Success stops being about how much you make and starts being about what each dollar makes possible.

These two dimensions form four financial profiles, as shown in Figure 6.2.

• *Busy Owner (Low Discipline, Money as the Goal): Everything feels urgent. There's no plan, just hustle. They chase every opportunity that looks like growth, but the profit vanishes before it compounds. With money as the goal, they focus on revenue instead of return, believing that more sales will eventually lead to more freedom. But without discipline, the money leaks, stress builds, and momentum never takes hold. It's a blur of activity with no direction. The business is running, but they're not moving forward. They're stuck in the work, stuck in the weeds, and stuck in the business.*

- *Working Rich (High Discipline, Money as the Goal): They've built a profitable business and created financial discipline, but they're still the engine that makes it run. Every dollar flows through them. They can afford the lifestyle, but don't have the time to enjoy it. It looks like success, but it's fragile. One bad year, and the high-wire act unravels. The business funds their life, but it takes their time.*

- *Cash Poor Entrepreneur (Low Discipline, Money as a Resource): They believe in building something better. They make good investment decisions, the kind that should compound, but without discipline, the returns never materialise. Every reinvestment feels like progress, but the results don't stick. The ideas are sound, the intent is strong, but the follow-through is missing. They're growing in size or revenue, but not in actual profit.*

- *Strategic Investor (High Discipline, Money as a Resource): They see money as a lever, one that, when applied with discipline, strengthens everything else. Profit is treated as a resource, not a reward. Every dollar has a job. Every investment decision is made with intent and followed through with rigour. They don't just pick the right opportunities, they make them count. They're not chasing growth, they're compounding value. The business fuels their lifestyle, their future investments, and their freedom.*

Understanding where you fall on this matrix is just the beginning. The real power comes from asking a deeper question: what system are you building around your financial decisions? Strategic Investors don't rely on instinct or hope; they create frameworks and systems that guide their thinking, shape their behaviour, and filter out distractions. That's what separates discipline from control. Discipline doesn't mean saying no to everything; it means knowing exactly what to say yes to, and then following through with rigour. Because when you treat money as a resource and invest with intention, you stop chasing success and start designing it.

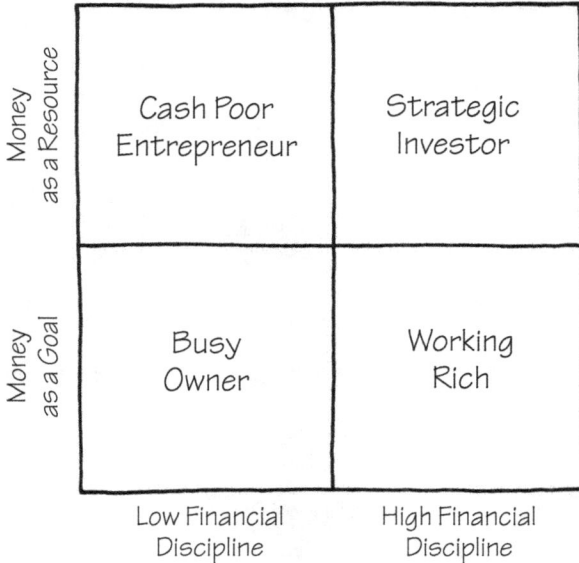

Figure 6.2 **The Strategic Investor Matrix**

But without that system, without clear financial rules and the discipline to follow them, even the most promising businesses can drift. And the danger is, drift does not always look like failure. In fact, it often looks like progress. Revenue climbs, the team grows and activity is everywhere. But as Figure 6.3 shows, what is happening beneath the surface often tells a very different story.

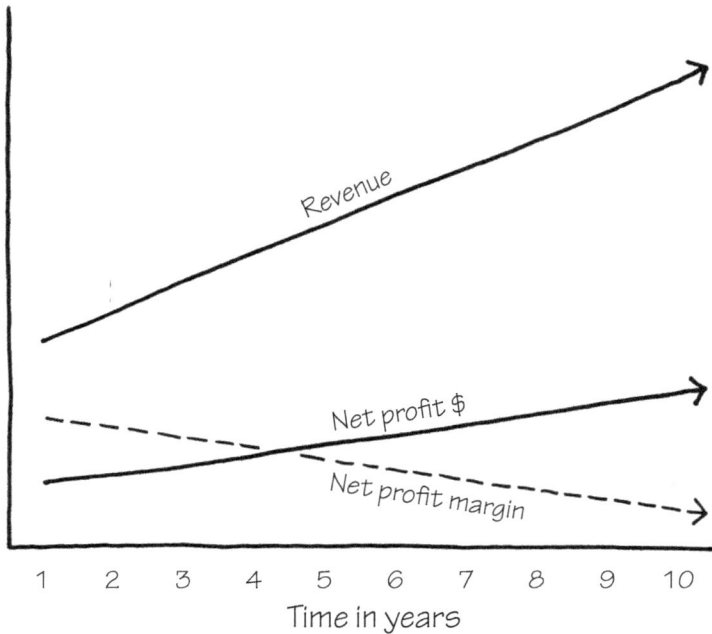

Figure 6.3 **Financial Drift**

While revenue rises steadily, net profit margin quietly erodes as overheads expand. The business delivers more but keeps less. And although net profit dollars may show some growth, it does so at a slowing pace, barely keeping up with the demands of a more complex business.

This is financial drift, a widening gap between effort and reward, complexity and control. And it is rarely just about the money. The root cause is usually upstream. When the team is not strong, the customers are not ideal or the offering is not compelling, no amount of financial discipline can hold the line. Weakness in any of those areas accelerates the drift, and the harder you push, the more fragile the business becomes.

That's why Strategic Investors go beyond financial thinking; they behave like strategic executors when it is time to act. Back in Chapter 1, we explored the leadership matrix with discipline on one axis and patience on the other. The strategic executor lives in the top right quadrant and is the behavioural opposite of the impulsive risk taker. Not fast, but focused. Not reactive, but rigorous.

They bring discipline not just to investment decisions, but to the execution that turns those investments into measurable outcomes. Whether the investment is in building a better team, attracting better customers, or refining the offering, the mindset stays the same: money is a resource, and every dollar must work. Strategic Investors apply financial discipline across the board, setting clear criteria, following through with rigour, and measuring returns over time. Because to them, better isn't just a vision; it's an investment that must deliver.

That's what gives the strategic executor their edge: they don't just manage money, they manage time. Every disciplined decision compounds. Each investment builds on the last, and over time, the business gets easier to run, not harder. That's how they earn compound interest, not just financially, but operationally. Their systems reinforce themselves. Their returns stack. Meanwhile, the impulsive risk taker burns energy chasing urgency and pays compound interest for the privilege. As Figure 6.4 shows, the disciplined and patient leader doesn't just build a business, they build momentum. And momentum, when compounded, becomes wealth.

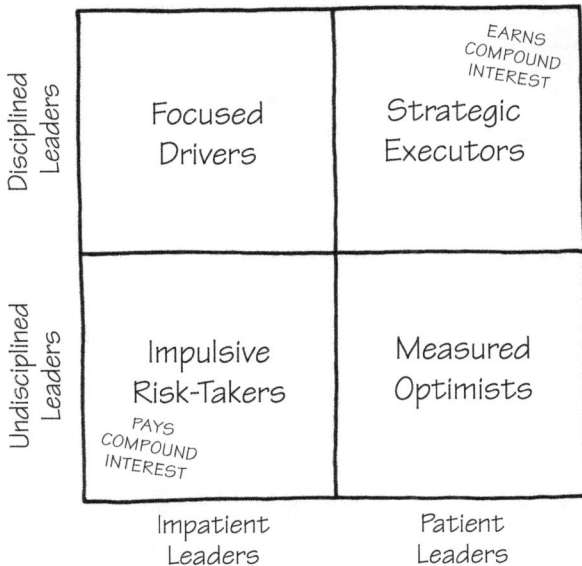

	Impatient Leaders	Patient Leaders
Disciplined Leaders	Focused Drivers	Strategic Executors *EARNS COMPOUND INTEREST*
Undisciplined Leaders	Impulsive Risk-Takers *PAYS COMPOUND INTEREST*	Measured Optimists

Figure 6.4 **Strategic Executors earn compound interest**

The Two Foundations of Better Financials

In the Strategic Investor Matrix, we explored two axes and two foundations that shape every financial outcome in an Owner Led Company: discipline and how you view money. Together, they form the system behind financial strength or drift. One determines how intentionally you allocate capital. The other determines whether that capital builds long-term value or just fuels more activity. Get either one wrong, and the business feels harder than it should. Get both right, and something powerful begins to happen: effort compounds.

We'll explore both foundations in this section, starting with the one that unlocks control: financial discipline. Because without it, even the best business model can spiral into chaos. The chart below outlines ten levels of discipline, from reactive chaos to structured control. Most Owner Led Companies land somewhere in the middle: they've outgrown instinct, but haven't yet installed a system. Budgets are loose, decisions are late, and financial data is more of a rearview mirror than a planning tool. But as Figure 6.5 shows, discipline isn't binary. It's built step by step, from basic visibility to full control. The businesses that reach the top don't just grow into it. They install it. Intentionally. Deliberately. One level at a time.

The following levels outline the practical journey, from no financial discipline to complete control, that every Owner Led Company must climb to build disciplined, durable financial systems.

> *Level 1 – There are no budgets or forecasting. All financial data is historical.*
> This is financial survival mode. You're flying blind, relying on instinct and past results with no forward view or structure.

> *Level 2 – There are quarterly and annual sales and profit targets.*
> There's a goal, but no data to back it. Targets are set, but often missed because no one owns the outcome or tracks the gap.

> *Level 3 – Income reporting is normalised at meetings.*

Reporting becomes routine, but impact is still inconsistent. The team sees the numbers, but they don't yet drive behaviour.

Level 4 – Income budgets are consistently achieved.
Now there's some rigour. Budgeting is tied to reality, and performance begins to align with the plan. People are starting to take it seriously.

Level 5 – All financial decisions are made before the year begins.
Budgeting isn't just about tracking; it's about intent. At this level, decisions are mapped before the year begins, and execution follows design, not emotion.

Level 6 – Budget variance is normalised in reports and meetings.
Leaders are trained to see, understand, and respond to variance. There's a culture of review, learning, and course correction.

Level 7 – Financial statements have a person assigned to each line item.
Accountability is distributed. Everyone knows who owns what financially and responsibility becomes shared, not centralised.

Level 8 – one or two KPIs are reported on weekly for each role / person.
The team is financially literate and focused. Every person knows what success looks like, and how their work, as outlined in their role scorecard, directly contributes to achieving those KPIs on a weekly basis.

Level 9 – There is an accurate 3-year cash-based rolling forecast.
Planning is long-range and dynamic. They don't just plan for next quarter; they engineer the next three years.

Level 10 – All spending and revenue budgets are consistently achieved.
This is the platform for freedom. When budgets perform like clockwork, leaders can focus on strategy, not survival and use profit as a resource, not a reward.

LEVEL 10 — All spending and revenue budgets are consistently achieved

LEVEL 9 — There is an accurate three-year cash-based rolling forecast

LEVEL 8 — One or two KPIs are reported on weekly for each role / person

LEVEL 7 — Financial statements have a person assigned to each line item

LEVEL 6 — Budget variance is normalised in reports and meetings

LEVEL 5 — All financial decisions are made before the year begins

LEVEL 4 — Income budgets are consistently achieved

LEVEL 3 — Income reporting is normalised at meetings

LEVEL 2 — There are quarterly and annual sales and profit targets

LEVEL 1 — There are no budgets or forecasting. All financial data is historical

Figure 6.5 **The Ten Levels of Financial Discipline**

Each level builds on the last. No shortcuts. Just structure, clarity, and intent, one step at a time.

So ask yourself: *which level is your business operating at today?* And what would it take to move just one level higher?

I once spoke with a business owner who proudly declared, 'We should be investing 10 per cent of our revenue into marketing.'

'Why?' I asked.

He paused. 'That's what good companies do.'

'According to who?' I replied.

There was another pause. 'Okay... let's go with 4 per cent.'

The problem? At that moment, the business was spending zero on marketing and making zero profit. No budget. No plan. Just an assumption, pulled from someone else's benchmarking playbook.

This is what financial drift looks like, not reckless spending, but reactive thinking. It feels like progress, but the numbers don't follow. Borrowed benchmarks. Decisions made in isolation from reality. Financial discipline isn't about copying what others do; it's about understanding what your business needs, why it needs it, and how it will pay off. Strategy without structure is just guesswork. And in this case, the right number wasn't 10 per cent, or even 4 per cent. It was a better question, followed by a smarter plan.

That conversation wasn't really about marketing. It was about mindset.

The owner wasn't treating money as a resource to be used intentionally; they were chasing a benchmark, hoping it would make the business feel more legitimate. That's what happens when money becomes the goal. You spend to prove something, not to build something. And when your thinking is off, the money doesn't build anything, it just disappears.

This is the second foundation behind better financials: how you view money. Some owners treat it as a scoreboard, a symbol of freedom or success. Others see it as fuel, a resource to be allocated, protected, and compounded. That mindset shift changes everything. In an Owner Led Company, money is more than just a means to an end; it's a tool to be managed with intention and care. Instead of spending $100, the goal is to grow it strategically, turning

$100 into $120, then $120 into $144, compounding value with every decision. This approach not only builds wealth but also creates the foundation for long-term, sustainable growth.

Together, these two foundations, financial discipline and viewing money as a resource, are what separate financial drift from financial momentum. One is about the rules you follow. The other is about why you follow them. Without discipline, you can't control outcomes. Without the right mindset, you won't pursue the right ones. But when you have both, every dollar works harder, every decision compounds, and every step builds toward something better. That's how Strategic Investors operate; they build better financials.

Building Better Financials

Your financials tell a story. Not just about the numbers, but about your mindset, your discipline, and the decisions you make every day. If your mindset treats money as a reward, you're likely to spend reactively and chase growth that doesn't stick. If your discipline is poor, you'll make decisions without structure and wonder why the returns never show up. But when you shift the mindset and apply discipline, everything changes. Better financials aren't built by doing more. They're built by improving what you already do, and doing it with clarity, intention, and control. The goal isn't to grow faster. It's to build a business that gets stronger every time it earns. It's not getting bigger. It's getting better.

Better financials are not built in the finance department; they are built through the decisions you make every day. A better team serving better customers with a better offering creates results. But wealth is built by what you do next. When you treat money as a resource and apply discipline to how you use it, each good decision creates the foundation for the next. Profit is not something you simply take out of the business; it is put to work with purpose. One smart investment strengthens another, and over time, momentum starts to build. Not from a single big win, but by doing the right things, in the right way, consistently.

In contrast to the Bigger Financials Doom Loop, the Better Financials Flywheel offers a roadmap for compounding returns and resilience over time. Based on Jim Collins' flywheel concept, this framework shows how discipline and mindset fuel momentum and how reinvesting into better teams, better customers, and better offerings powers a stronger, more valuable business with every rotation.

Here's how the Better Financials Flywheel shown in Figure 6.5 works:

1 *Invest in Better Teams, Customers, and Offerings*

   Building better financials starts by putting your resources where they create the greatest long-term value. Not everything needs to grow, but the areas that strengthen your business must. Invest where you build capability, deepen loyalty and create a distinct advantage because these are the foundations that drive sustainable financial results.

2 *Maximise Results Using the Better Teams, Customers & Offerings Approach*

   With those investments in place, execution sharpens, productivity increases, and results improve, without more effort. You begin to do less, but better. And the return on energy, time, and capital compounds.

3 *Generate Superior Business Returns*

   With better inputs and better execution, the right outcomes follow. Margins improve. Cash flow becomes more predictable. The business starts to grow on the inside, not just the outside. These aren't one-off gains; they are repeatable results that strengthen the business and create the capacity for further investment. Each financial improvement feeds the next, building momentum and generating returns that compound over time.

4   *Apply Disciplined Investment Criteria Using*
the Money-as-a-Resource Mindset

With surplus capital, you now face a choice: spend it, or compound it. Strategic Investors don't guess, they use rules. Instead of reacting to every opportunity, they allocate based on return, timing, and risk. Every dollar has a job. You don't spend to get bigger; you invest for progress.

5   *Reinvest One-Third of Returns Back to the Business*
(Other Two-Thirds to External Assets, Lifestyle)

The final step is to intentionally allocate returns three ways, reinvesting into the business, funding your lifestyle, and building external wealth. One portion strengthens the system. The rest fuels the life you're building outside it. The balance may shift year to year, but the principle stays the same: invest across all three domains, on purpose.

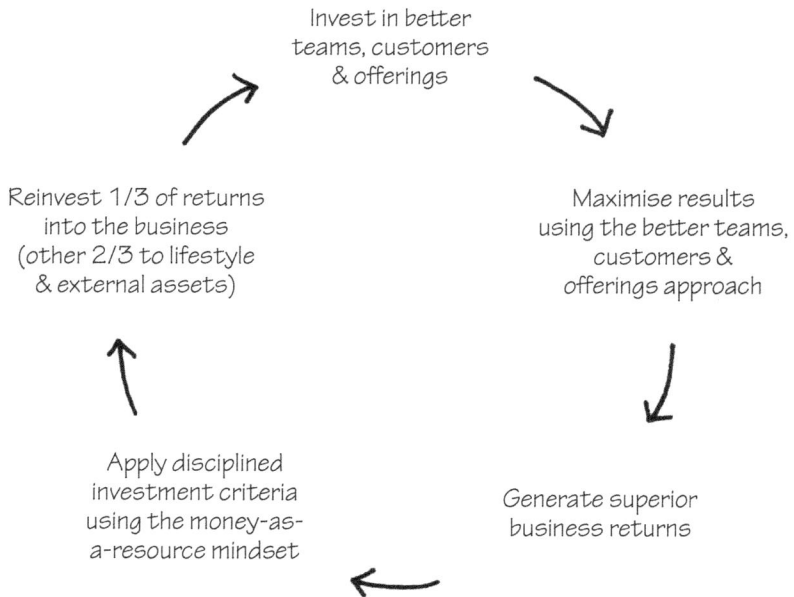

Invest in better
teams, customers
& offerings

Reinvest 1/3 of returns
into the business
(other 2/3 to lifestyle
& external assets)

Maximise results
using the better teams,
customers &
offerings approach

Apply disciplined
investment criteria
using the money-as-
a-resource mindset

Generate superior
business returns

Each investment creates a compounding cash on cash return
and therefore you can transition to more of an investor over time

Figure 6.6 **The Better Financials Flywheel**

Each time around, returns improve. Decisions get sharper. Risk decreases. And your business gets stronger without becoming harder. With each spin of the flywheel, capital becomes more productive, decisions become more disciplined, and wealth builds on itself, by design.

A note about the reinvesting thirds.

One of the biggest traps for Owner Led Companies is putting every dollar back into the business. It feels responsible, even noble. But without a system or a stop point, that cycle never ends. The owner stays stuck, funding the growth, carrying the risk, and never realising the reward. Others swing the other way. They take too much, too soon. They build a lifestyle the business can't sustain or take on unnecessary debt that chokes future flexibility. In both cases, it's not strategy, it's drift.

And this is where the financial story becomes personal. Because what you do with that profit, how you allocate it, protect it, and deploy it, is ultimately what shapes your life. It's not just about growing a business that performs well on paper. It's about building a business that funds the life you want to live, not one that owns you.

When you think like a Strategic Investor, you stop chasing growth for its own sake. You start building by design. As shown in Figure 6.7, every dollar earned creates a deliberate choice across three areas: reinvestment in the business, building external assets and supporting your lifestyle. A portion goes back into the business so you can keep getting better. A portion fuels your personal lifestyle, so you can enjoy the benefits of your effort now, not one day. And a portion goes toward external assets that build wealth independently of your business, creating security and freedom beyond the day-to-day operations.

This balance is what separates Owner Led Companies that are resilient, scalable, and valuable from those that feel like a trap. Rather than just a financial model, it's a life model. The reinvesting thirds principle matters because it's not about a fixed formula; it's about applying both financial discipline and the money-as-a-resource mindset.

One year, you might reinvest 15 per cent back into the business, allocate 60 per cent toward building external wealth, and take 25 per cent to enjoy life today. The next year, those numbers might shift. What matters is that you're investing intentionally across all three domains: business strength, personal wealth, and lifestyle freedom. Each one plays a role in long-term success. While tax considerations will always shape how you apply this principle, the real point is this: wealth is not just what stays in the business; it is what flows from it, by design. And when you separate those returns and build momentum across all four flywheels, you can begin to use that money and freedom to build your better life, by design.

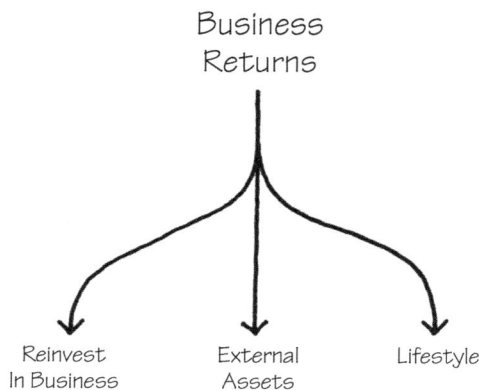

Figure 6.7 **The Reinvesting Thirds Framework**

The Better Financials Assessment

Building better financials is about using what you earn with discipline and intent. Better Owner Led Companies don't just make money, they manage it wisely. Use the five questions below to assess whether your current financial mindset and practices are compounding long-term strength or quietly drifting toward fragility. If you can't confidently answer 'yes' with an 8/10 or higher rating, it's a signal that your financial system may need to evolve to create wealth by design, not by accident.

- *Do you treat money in the business as a resource to allocate with discipline, not a reward to spend, and would you rate your financial mindset at 8/10 or higher?*

- *Do you apply disciplined investment criteria based on return, timing, and risk, rather than reacting to opportunities, and would you confidently rate that approach at 8/10 or higher?*

- *Do you have a clear and intentional system for deciding how much profit stays in the business, how much supports your lifestyle, and how much goes to external assets, and would you confidently rate that system at 8/10 or higher?*

- *Are your reinvestments strengthening the parts of the business that create long-term value, like your people, customers, and offerings, and would you confidently rate your focus at 8/10 or higher?*

- *Do you track whether previous reinvestments are delivering measurable returns, and would you confidently rate that discipline at 8/10 or higher?*

Better financials aren't just about margins or management reports; they're about freedom. When you treat money as a resource and apply discipline to how it's earned, allocated, and reinvested, you take control of your future in a way most Owner Led Companies never do. You're not just reacting to opportunity or patching problems with spending. You're investing in what truly matters. And when those investments compound, your business becomes more profitable, more resilient, and more valuable, without the constant anxiety that growth might collapse under its own weight.

Because when all four flywheels are turning, team, customers, offering, and financials, the business starts working for you, not the other way around. You're compounding momentum. You're building wealth. And most importantly, you're creating the freedom to live life on your terms.

In the next chapter, we'll explore how to use that strength and freedom to build not just a better business, but your better life, by design.

CHAPTER 7

Your Better Life,
By Design

*'People are working so hard to climb the ladder
of success only to find that it was leaning against
the wrong wall when they get there.'*
DR STEPHEN COVEY

From Building a Better Business to Building a Better Life

For years, you've been stuck in the cycle of business grind, never truly able to see beyond it. But now, something has shifted. You're beginning to feel that freedom, the real kind, where business doesn't just consume you but propels you toward a life of fulfilment.

You've read the last few chapters with a growing sense of clarity, maybe even momentum. After exploring better teams, customers, offerings, and financials, you might be seeing that true freedom comes not from growth alone, but from intentional, meaningful choices. For the first time in years, the idea of freedom doesn't feel abstract. It feels possible. Tangible. Like something you're beginning to believe you could actually earn. Not by chasing more, but by choosing better. As each flywheel came into focus—team, customers, offering, financials—you began to feel the pull of a different path. A better one. One that doesn't just fix the business but might finally lead to the life that always felt just out of reach.

You didn't start your business to be consumed by it. You started it for freedom. For a life that was truly yours. But somewhere along the way, the numbers, the pressure, and the constant hustle swallowed your dream. You're tired of just building. You want to live. To walk into your home at the end of the day with energy. To truly be present for your family and not feel like you're running on empty.

For years, you believed owning a business would lead to ultimate freedom, but you soon realised that without structure, it becomes chaos. The harder you pushed, the further that freedom slipped away from you. But now, you're about to discover how to catch it for good.

In Chapter 1, we saw how freedom, without direction, often leads to distraction. Without discipline and patience, you end up chasing everything and making little real progress. But now, with structure in place and four flywheels turning, freedom feels different. You have the confidence to stay disciplined on what works and the patience to let meaningful progress take shape. And for the first time, you can choose your path deliberately. With purpose. By design.

The life you've been chasing, the one that feels truly yours, begins now. It starts with these five areas. And through them, you'll design the life you've always wanted.

Healthy

Your health is the foundation of a better life by design. It's about living as healthily and actively as possible for as long as possible. Without physical endurance and mental clarity, you can't fully engage with any of the other areas of life. Health isn't something to wait to fix when it's broken. It's something to proactively maintain, investing in your energy, mental clarity, and vitality so you can live the life you want on your own terms. Remember, the healthy person wants 100 things, the sick person wants 1 thing.

Wealthy

Wealth is central to a better life by design. By investing beyond the business, you build wealth that stands on its own, providing the freedom to live life on your terms. Wealth is about leveraging your financial resources to create long-term security, allowing you to enjoy time, experiences, and opportunities without worry. It's about making your money work for you, building a life where financial freedom supports your vision for the future.

Wise

Wisdom is how you become a better version of yourself: constantly learning, growing, and applying new insights. It's about actively seeking knowledge and wisdom before challenges arise so you're ready to face anything that comes your way. Set wisdom goals, such as reading, finding mentors, or actively seeking new experiences to broaden your perspective. For example, one of my own wisdom goals is to travel to Antarctica.

Happy

Happiness is about purpose and fulfilment. It's the direction you
choose to travel in life and the people you travel with. It's about
doing the things that bring you joy and intentionally curating a life
of meaning. Happiness is a choice you make every day, a decision
to live with intention and purpose.

Great Family

A great family enhances the lives of its members by
creating a supportive network where everyone thrives. Whether it
is your immediate family, extended family or whatever you define
as family, the goal is to strengthen these bonds steadily, through
small, consistent actions over time. As a leader in your family, you
are in a unique position to shape its future. Think of your family
like building a cathedral. Cathedrals were not built in a day; they
took years, sometimes generations, with each stone carefully
placed to create something lasting and beautiful. In the same
way, every conversation, shared experience and family tradition
you invest in becomes part of a strong foundation. Over the years,
these moments create a family culture that stands resilient and
meaningful for those who come after you. A great family is not
built by accident or only in times of crisis. It is built deliberately,
through care, effort and intention.

These five areas are the foundation of a life designed with purpose. We'll
explore them all in this chapter.

Back in 2007, I was a member of Entrepreneurs Organization and
met monthly with a forum group of peers. It was during that time that
I developed a personal goal-setting tool that became the foundation for
this chapter. The original framework focused on Healthy, Wealthy, and
Wise. But after a few years, it became clear that something was missing.
Without Happiness and Great Family, the goals felt incomplete. So I added
those too. Since then, I've used and refined this model with many leaders

across Australia and New Zealand. The structure has evolved, but the intent remains the same: to help you design a better life, one that feels fulfilled, intentional, and whole.

At a lunch recently, my friend Jay recalled how we started this exercise nearly twenty years ago. He set his goals using this framework, updating them every year. 'It's wild... every goal I set, I hit,' he told me. 'But more than that, I can see how I grew in all five areas, and how they supported each other.' His success wasn't accidental. It came from doing the work, designing a better life, consistently, year after year.

That's the opportunity ahead of you now: to take this same structure and shape it to fit your life, so the next chapter of your journey feels more aligned, more rewarding, and uniquely yours.

The five areas are interdependent. When one is missing, the whole structure falters. To achieve your full potential, each area must be nurtured. Health, wealth, wisdom, happiness, and family come together to form the foundation of a life by design. Without all five, you can't reach self-actualisation. When all five areas are aligned, you create a life that feels intentional, fulfilled, and meaningful.

For the first time, you're not just building a business. You're designing a life that reflects your deepest values. To make that life real, we begin with health, the foundation that supports everything else. Without health, nothing else can thrive. Let's explore how to nurture your body and mind so you can create the life you truly desire.

Healthy

'The highest correlation of Fortune 500 CEOs is not race, it's not gender, it's not the university they went to, it's that they exercise 5 times a week'
SCOTT GALLOWAY

Health isn't just about how long you live. It's about how well you live. It forms the foundation for everything else. When you're healthy, you can engage fully in all areas of life. Without health, the vitality of your wealth, wisdom, happiness and family is at risk. Freedom means living the most fulfilling life you can, for as long as possible. That's where healthspan comes in. It refers to the number of years you live in optimal health, feeling strong, energised and capable of engaging in the activities you love, rather than simply how long you live. It's what allows you to thrive.

Healthspan is not maintained by one good decision. It is earned through consistency over time. When you eat well, sleep well and exercise regularly, you build endurance. In the short term, endurance gives you the energy, focus and stability to show up fully each day. Over time, it becomes the strength that protects your healthspan, allowing you to stay active, resilient and capable for longer. This applies not just to your body, but to your mind as well. Physical endurance keeps you strong and mobile. Mental endurance helps you stay clear-headed, emotionally steady and able to thrive under pressure. Together, they give you the capacity to live well, not just longer. To optimise your healthspan.

Physical & Mental Endurance

As shown in Figure 7.1, physical endurance is supported by a balance of three key factors: exercise, nutrition and rest. These are not one-time choices. They are ongoing investments in your energy, strength and clarity. When these three elements are in balance, you build the stamina needed to stay healthy and active for longer. That is how you protect and extend your healthspan and give yourself the foundation to thrive in every other part of life.

Let's take a closer look at how exercise, nutrition and rest each contribute to your physical endurance and overall healthspan.

Exercise is crucial for maintaining long-term health and longevity. Dr. Peter Attia stresses the importance of strength, stability, and flexibility, not just for cardiovascular fitness, but for preserving muscle mass and functional mobility as we age. Regular resistance training and other forms of exercise help combat chronic diseases such as atherosclerosis, cancer, and type 2 diabetes, contributing to a healthier, longer life.

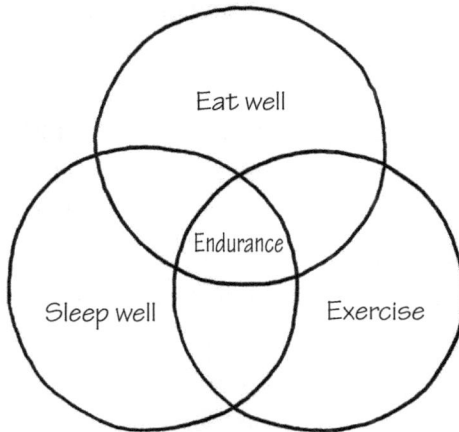

Figure 7.1 **Physical Endurance**

Nutrition supports long-term health by impacting immediate bodily function and resilience to disease. Dr. Casey Means emphasises that 'eating whole, nutrient-dense foods and reducing processed foods is the cornerstone of a healthy lifestyle.' A diet rich in low-inflammatory, low-glycaemic foods, fibre, healthy fats, and antioxidants supports metabolic health and prevents chronic conditions. By prioritising these foods, you nourish your body for sustained energy, setting the foundation for a thriving life.

Rest is essential for physical and mental recovery. Dr. Attia describes sleep as 'the most underappreciated pillar of health.' Consistent, quality sleep (7-9 hours per night) is crucial for immune function, mental clarity, emotional stability, and physical repair. Prioritising rest helps your body regenerate, enhances cognitive performance, and supports your healthspan, so you can thrive in the short and long term.

Mental endurance is just as important as physical endurance. It is what helps you stay grounded, emotionally steady and focused through life's inevitable challenges. As shown in Figure 7.2, mental endurance is supported by three essential elements: something to do (purposeful engagement), someone to love (social connection), and something to look forward to (hope and anticipation). Together, these elements strengthen your ability to remain resilient and fulfilled across every area of life.

Having something to do is the first and most active ingredient in mental resilience. It is not just about staying busy, but about engaging in meaningful tasks and goals that align with your values and passions. As Viktor Frankl wrote in *Man's Search for Meaning*, 'Those who have a why to live, can bear almost any how.' Research confirms that purpose-driven activities such as work, hobbies, or volunteering reduce stress, enhance well-being, and foster a sense of accomplishment. For business owners especially, it is essential to stay meaningfully engaged in work and life. Purpose is not static; it evolves, so finding new ways to contribute and grow is vital to long-term fulfilment.

Closely tied to that sense of purpose is the need for someone to love. We are social beings, and strong relationships are a core part of mental wellbeing. Emotional connection provides a sense of safety and belonging that helps us manage stress and navigate adversity. Dr. John Cacioppo's research on loneliness shows that social isolation increases stress and raises the risk of poor health outcomes. By contrast, strong relationships, whether with family, friends or a partner, create a support system that enhances emotional resilience and contributes to your overall healthspan.

Finally, something to look forward to gives us emotional momentum. Anticipating a positive event activates the brain's reward system, helping us stay motivated through difficult or repetitive seasons. Whether it is a holiday, a personal milestone or a new project, having something on the horizon gives meaning to the present. Studies show that anticipation improves mood, reduces stress and boosts mental resilience. When we have something to look forward to, we are better equipped to stay engaged and keep pursuing our long-term goals.

Purpose, connection and hope build the mental endurance you need to stay resilient over time. When these elements are nurtured alongside physical health, they give you the strength to stay focused, engaged and emotionally steady, no matter what life brings. You aren't just protecting your mind or your body. You're protecting your ability to live with clarity, energy and joy.

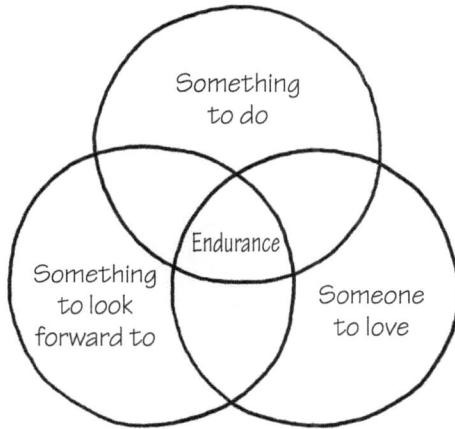

Figure 7.2 **Mental Endurance**

Healthspan vs Lifespan

This is the difference between lifespan and healthspan. It's not about how long you live, but how well you live in the years that matter most. Your healthspan is shaped by both physical and mental endurance, and the choices you make today directly impact how long you will stay strong, capable and independent. A longer healthspan means more years doing what you love, with the people you love, in the way you choose.

As shown in Figure 7.3, there are three approaches to health and longevity. The first, No Intervention, represents a life where no active effort is made to manage health, leading to a gradual decline over time. Medicine 2, a reactive approach, begins to show the effects of chronic diseases such as heart disease and type 2 diabetes from the early 40s onward, leading to diminishing quality of life even if lifespan is extended. In contrast, Medicine 3 is proactive. By focusing on prevention, slowing ageing, and preventing chronic conditions, it helps preserve both physical and mental endurance and ensures a vibrant life well into old age. Medicine 3 prioritises long-term vitality and health rather than simply managing illness. This is why it is essential to proactively plan a Better Life by Design, beginning with the Healthy area. By prioritising physical and mental endurance, we can extend our healthspan and avoid the trap of reactive healthcare and the decline in quality of life.

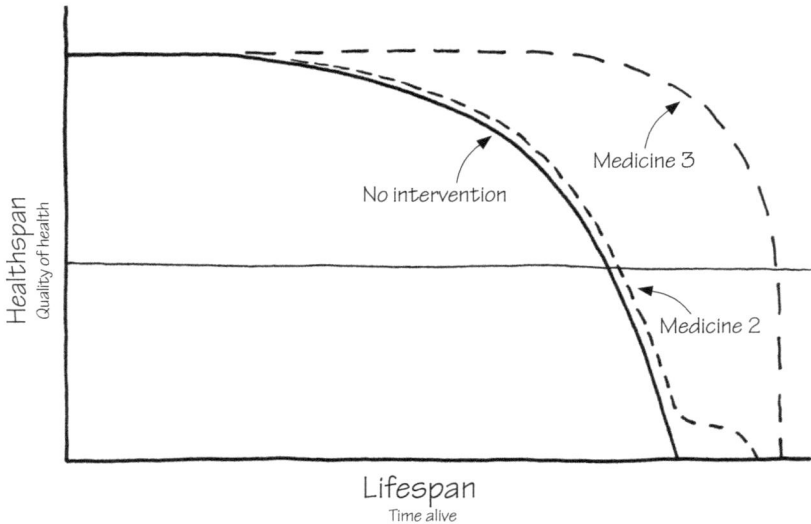

Figure 7.3 **Healthspan vs Lifespan**

Designing your Healthy Life

As we move forward, we'll be working through the Better Life, by Design Worksheet together. This worksheet will serve as your roadmap for defining and tracking your health, wealth, wisdom, happiness, and family goals over the long term. It's a tool to help you design your life with intention—ensuring that every step you take brings you closer to the life you envision.

At the beginning of this section, take a look at the worksheet (shown in Figure 7.4) as it outlines the key areas we'll explore: health, wealth, wisdom, happiness, and family. We will revisit this worksheet throughout the chapter, setting goals and actions for each of these areas. By the end, you'll have a clear, actionable plan to move forward with confidence.

Healthy	Wealthy	Wise	Happy	Great Family
OVERALL GOAL	OVERALL GOAL	OVERALL GOAL	OVERALL GOAL	OVERALL GOAL
ACTIONS & MEASURES	ACTIONS & MEASURES	ACTIONS & MEASURES	ACTIONS & MEASURES	ACTIONS & MEASURES
10 YEAR	10 YEAR	10 YEAR	10 YEAR	10 YEAR
3 YEAR	3 YEAR	3 YEAR	3 YEAR	3 YEAR
1 YEAR	1 YEAR	1 YEAR	1 YEAR	1 YEAR
3 MONTHS	3 MONTHS	3 MONTHS	3 MONTHS	3 MONTHS

Figure 7.4 Better Life, By Design Worksheet

You can download the full Better Life, by Design Worksheet at *evolutionpartners.com.au*. This will allow you to fill it out as we go along, making it an interactive part of your journey towards a better, more intentional life.

Now that we've explored the importance of health and endurance, let's focus on setting your health goals, which will serve as the cornerstone of your Better Life by Design. Start by defining what a healthy life looks like for you. Consider factors like longevity, vitality, freedom from illness, and the energy to enjoy all aspects of life.

Once you've reflected on these elements, write your timeless health goal. Choose a sentence that captures how you want to feel and function at every stage of life. This goal will guide your decisions and actions moving forward. For example, my health goal is: 'To live a long, healthy life free from disease and unnecessary pain.' All my major and minor goals, as well as my daily activities, cascade from this central health goal, ensuring that every action I take aligns with this vision.

By defining your health goal clearly, you create a strong foundation for the actions you'll take in the coming sections. This goal ensures your physical, mental, and emotional well-being are aligned with the life you want to create and helps you stay focused on what matters most.

To achieve your health goal, start by defining specific actions you will take and how you will measure your progress.

List 5 to 10 actions and measures that you will regularly undertake to achieve your health goal. Actions are what you must do to achieve the goal, and measures are how you track that action. For example, if one action is cardio exercise, the measure would be 'cardio hours.' Later, when setting your goals, you might decide to aim for 4 cardio hours per week in one year.

Examples might include cardio hours, strength training, sleep hours, annual blood tests, tracking healthy or unhealthy food intake, weight, or monitoring alcohol consumption. You might track your resting heart rate, VO2 max, or push-up count as strength benchmarks. Remember, these actions should work for you. For instance, swimming laps might not be ideal for me, but another activity could be.

By defining these actions and measurable indicators, you'll create a clear, actionable plan to follow and tangible ways to track your progress. Use the Better Life, By Design Worksheet to document your actions and measures, ensuring they align with your long-term health vision.

Now that you've set your overall health goal and defined your actions and measures, it's time to break them down into specific, time-based goals.

Start with your 10-year goals. These long-term milestones are directly informed by the actions and measures you've outlined. Then, create your 3-year, 1-year, and 90-day goals. Each period represents a stepping stone, helping you evolve and maintain your long-term health vision, one that embodies how you want to feel at every stage of life.

For reference, see Figure 7.5, which displays an example of the health section of the Better Life, By Design Worksheet. This diagram outlines how to structure your health goals across multiple timeframes (10-year, 3-year, 1-year, and 90-day), helping you track and measure your progress as you move toward your ultimate health goal.

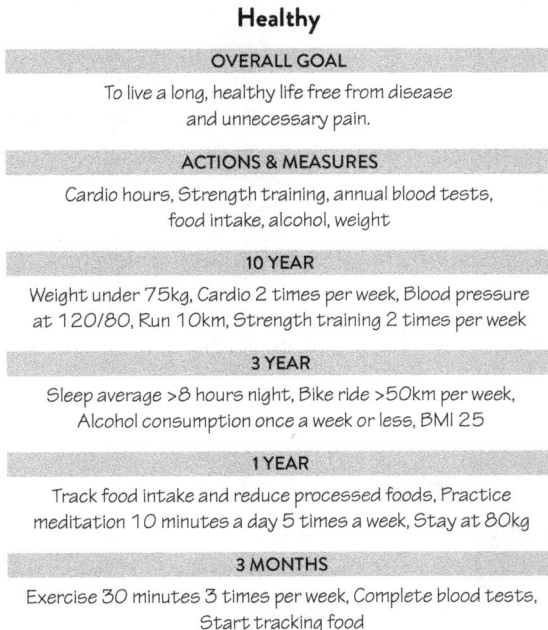

Healthy

OVERALL GOAL

To live a long, healthy life free from disease and unnecessary pain.

ACTIONS & MEASURES

Cardio hours, Strength training, annual blood tests, food intake, alcohol, weight

10 YEAR

Weight under 75kg, Cardio 2 times per week, Blood pressure at 120/80, Run 10km, Strength training 2 times per week

3 YEAR

Sleep average >8 hours night, Bike ride >50km per week, Alcohol consumption once a week or less, BMI 25

1 YEAR

Track food intake and reduce processed foods, Practice meditation 10 minutes a day 5 times a week, Stay at 80kg

3 MONTHS

Exercise 30 minutes 3 times per week, Complete blood tests, Start tracking food

Figure 7.5 **Healthy section, Better Life, By Design Worksheet example**

These are your personal health goals, so feel free to use the examples provided in Figure 7.5 as a guide, but remember, they are just examples. Your own goals should reflect your unique priorities, challenges, and vision for health. By documenting your goals this way, you will have a clear roadmap to follow, ensuring that each action you take aligns with your vision for lasting health.

The Better Health, By Design Assessment

Here are three questions to help you assess where you currently stand on health in your Better Life, By Design. Reflect on each one and rate yourself honestly. This exercise will give you a clearer picture of how well you're following through on your health commitments and highlight areas that may need fine-tuning to align with your long-term health vision.

- *Have you clearly defined your long-term health goal, and would you confidently rate your progress toward that goal at 8/10 or higher?*

- *Are you consistently taking actions that support both your physical and mental endurance? Would you rate your consistency and follow-through at 8 out of 10 or higher?*

- *How well are you balancing physical endurance (exercise, nutrition, sleep) with mental endurance (purpose, social connection, anticipation), and would you confidently rate your balance at 8/10 or higher?*

Health is the foundation for success in all areas of your life, including wealth, wisdom, family, and happiness. Without it, none of the other areas can truly thrive. Now that you have a clear plan in place for your health, we can turn our attention to the next critical area: wealth. This is where we build and manage the resources that will support your freedom and help you achieve your goals. Let's dive into how you can design a prosperous and sustainable financial future.

Wealthy

'Poverty stops the best minds in their tracks'
VINCENT VAN GOGH

'When does it all end? How many yachts can you water ski behind?'
BUD FOX ASKING GORDON GEKKO IN THE MOVIE WALL STREET

Wealth is the fuel for freedom.

It gives you the power to choose how you live, not just how you work. When you're wealthy, you're not trapped by your business or your calendar. You have time for the people you love, space for the things that matter, and the confidence that your future is secure. Wealth gives you options. Not just to grow, but to stop. Not just to earn, but to live. And yet, for many owners, wealth never arrives because it's trapped inside the business, never converted into real financial freedom. True wealth isn't revenue or valuation. It's the ability to live life on your own terms, for as long as you choose.

You already understand how to treat money as a resource inside the business. In Chapter 6, we explored how to allocate profit with discipline, using clear rules to generate returns over time. Now it's time to apply that same mindset to your personal finances. Personal wealth isn't something you chase once and then forget. It is built through small, consistent decisions by extracting money from the business, resisting lifestyle creep, and investing in assets that compound over time. As Greg Crabtree puts it, if you own a cow, which represents your business, you can either have milk every day or have one barbecue. The intent is to have milk every day, so you can live the lifestyle you want and build wealth in assets outside the business. You still need a clear target for what enough looks like, but the mindset continues. You keep treating money as a resource, growing it with intention, so it supports the life you want without costing you the life you have.

When it comes to building wealth outside your business, not all investments are created equal. Some returns come with hidden costs, requiring more time, more energy, and more stress than they're worth. You're already running a business, so you don't need another job disguised as a portfolio. The key is to choose investments that not only offer a return but also align with the life you want to live.

Figure 7.6 shows how different types of personal investments compare, based on emotional load and expected return. Emotional load refers to the time involvement, decision fatigue, and the personal risk you carry, especially if debt is involved.

While some of these may not line up with your personal experience (maybe your uncle made a fortune with direct shares, or you're convinced residential property should be valued differently), the point is not precision; it's perspective. Every investment must be assessed based on how it fits your personal situation. The goal isn't always the highest return, but the investment that supports the life you want without disrupting the one you already have.

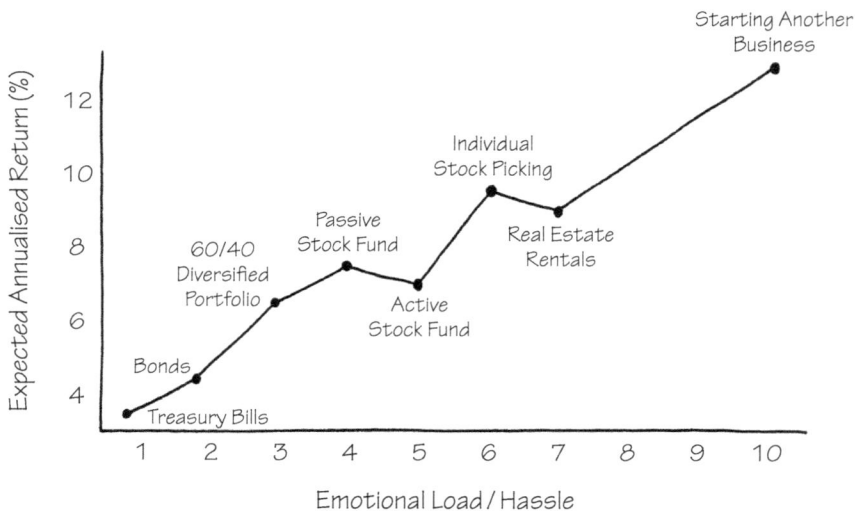

Figure 7.6 **Emotional Load vs Expected Return of Personal Investments**

When you apply the money-as-a-resource mindset to your personal finances, four areas matter most:

- *Asset Value – The measure of how much you've converted from business success into long-term wealth. This is your financial foundation.*

- *Passive Income – What your investments earn without your active involvement: like dividends, rent, or interest. It's income that works even when you don't, and it forms the backbone of long-term financial freedom.*

- *Cashflow – Your total money movement: how much actually hits your account each month, minus what goes out. It's not just what you earn, but how reliably it funds your lifestyle.*

- *Debt & Risk Management – The strategies that preserve what you've built. By controlling liabilities and managing exposure, you stay in command.*

These aren't just technical terms. They are the real levers of personal wealth, and most owners already have the discipline to master them. Now it's just about applying that discipline to your own life.

You can't build personal wealth without first defining what it means to you. And for that, you need a number. For some, it's a target for passive income. For others, it's a total net worth, or the monthly cashflow required to live comfortably without relying on the business. There's no right answer, only that it's the right answer for you. Until you name it, you're just guessing. But once you define that number, it gives you something powerful: clarity about where you're heading, confidence in the decisions you're making, and the peace of mind that comes from knowing you're on track. That number becomes your anchor. It shows you what to aim for, and it helps you decide what to do next. That's the first step in designing personal wealth that supports your life, not competes with it.

Wealthy

OVERALL GOAL

To build a cathedral balance sheet which is impenetrable with
positive liquidity

ACTIONS & MEASURES

Income, Asset Growth,
Cashflow, Debt

10 YEAR

$ 1m passive income, $ 20m external assets,
All assets cashflow postive, <$ 5m debt

3 YEAR

$ 200k passive income, $ 5m external assets,
<$ 500k negative cashflow, <$ 4m debt

1 YEAR

$ 50k passive income, $ 3m external assets,
$ 4.5m debt

3 MONTHS

Sell North st, Invest $ 100k into syndicate,
Stop the cash losses at Quinland

Figure 7.7 **Wealthy section, Better Life, By Design Worksheet example**

Designing your Wealthy Life

Now it's time to make that number tangible. In the *Better Life, By Design*
worksheet, you'll start by capturing your overall wealth goal, something that
reflects how you want money to work for you, not just in your business but
in life. For example, in Figure 7.7, the goal is to build a 'cathedral balance
sheet,' a strong, enduring financial position with positive liquidity at its
core. Once your goal is clear, you'll define the actions and measures that will
support it. These might include tracking income, growing external assets,
improving cashflow, or reducing personal debt. From there, you'll break your
wealth journey into achievable milestones: a 10-year target like $1 million in
passive income, a 3-year goal such as $5 million in external assets, a 1-year
goal, and a 90-day goal. That last piece matters. In the example, it includes
specific short-term actions such as selling an underperforming asset or

investing into a new syndicate to move the plan forward immediately. This process turns your financial vision into structure. Just as you applied discipline and structure to your business investments in Chapter 6, now you'll do the same in your personal life. From the big picture to the next 90 days, you're designing a wealth strategy that supports your life by design.

The Better Wealth, By Design Assessment

Here are three questions to help you assess where you currently stand on wealth in your Better Life, By Design. Reflect on each one and rate yourself honestly. This quick self-check will give you a clearer picture of how intentionally you're building personal wealth, and where small adjustments could help you better align with your long-term financial vision.

- *Have you clearly defined your long-term personal wealth goal, and would you confidently rate your progress at 8/10 or higher?*

- *Are you consistently extracting surplus from the business and investing it wisely, using clear rules? Would you rate your focus on this at 8/10 or higher?*

- *How well are you actively balancing the key levers of personal wealth: growing assets, building income, managing cashflow, and controlling debt? Would you confidently rate that balance at 8 out of 10 or higher?*

Wealth is the fuel that powers your life by design, giving you the freedom to make choices, the confidence to take control, and the resources to support what matters most. Without it, your goals stay out of reach, no matter how clear your vision is. Now that you've built a plan to grow your wealth with purpose, it's time to turn to the next critical area: wisdom. This is where you become a better version of yourself, through learning, reflection, and growth. Let's explore how you can design a life that isn't just rich in resources, but rich in perspective.

Wise

*'Experience is the hardest kind of teacher. It gives you
the test first and the lesson afterward.'*
OSCAR WILDE

Wisdom isn't just about what you know. It's about how you grow. It's the ability to think clearly, make better decisions, and become a better version of yourself over time. When you're wise, you don't just react. You reflect. You pause, ask better questions, and bring perspective to problems that would rattle others. The emotional reward of wisdom is confidence and calm decision-making. The unwise are certain they've figured it all out. The wise are certain they haven't. Without wisdom, you risk becoming frozen in old patterns, limited by past mistakes, or overly confident in your own ideas. Wisdom isn't something you stumble into. It's something you build. And the most effective leaders curate it with intention.

Not all learners are earners. But all earners are learners. The unwise pay the price of not learning. They repeat the same mistakes, run the same failing playbook, or miss the lesson that would have changed everything. Too many owners rely on lived experience as their primary teacher. But learning from your own mistakes is the most expensive way to grow. Learning from others is faster, safer, and smarter. It's what wise leaders do on purpose.

The barriers to wisdom aren't usually intellectual. They're personal. It might be ego, the belief that you already know enough. It might be time, the sense that learning is a luxury you can't afford. Or it might simply be that no one has shown you how to build a system that makes growth easier. Wisdom doesn't arrive by accident. It shows up when you make space for it consistently and create rhythms that keep you learning on purpose.

In our work with leadership teams, we ask every member to set a personal professional development goal each quarter, usually a book they commit to reading. It sounds simple, but it creates momentum. Over time, the smartest teams become wiser together. Why? Because wisdom

compounds. Not just for the individual, but for the whole organisation.
In your life by design, there are three core levers that help wisdom grow:

- *Curated Learning: Books, courses, conversations, mentors. This is wisdom you choose, like picking a book on pricing strategy because your margins are under pressure or learning about becoming a better parent.*

- *Lived Experience: Not just what you've been through, but what you've learned from it. Think of the insight that came from a failed hire or a tough conversation you finally had. It's also about seeking new, intentional experiences, like visiting companies in your industry overseas to learn how they operate.*

- *Self-Reflection: Journaling, thinking time, asking 'What is this teaching me?' It's the bridge between doing and growing, like taking 15 minutes on Friday to reflect on what that week taught you.*

Each lever strengthens the others. Reflection makes learning stick. Experience gives learning context. Curation ensures experience leads somewhere useful. These levers don't activate themselves. They must be chosen. And when they are, they compound, building the perspective, clarity, and emotional stability that allow you to lead wisely and live by design.

Designing your Wise Life

You've now seen how wisdom grows through curated learning, lived experience, and reflection. Now that you understand where wisdom comes from and how it compounds over time, it's time to turn that intention into structure.

In the Better Life, By Design worksheet, you'll define a clear wisdom goal, set actionable steps to support it, and outline time-based milestones to track your progress. The worksheet helps you structure your wisdom goals, as shown in Figure 7.8.

Wise

OVERALL GOAL
To become a better version of myself through intentional growth

ACTIONS & MEASURES
Books read per quarter, journaling frequency, number of mentors engaged, hours invested in structured learning

10 YEAR
Complete 100 meaningful books or teachings. Become a source of wisdom for others

3 YEAR
Attend 3 retreats, build a structured reading habit, engage a coach or mentor, and facilitate a learning session within your team.

1 YEAR
Read 12 books aligned with areas requiring growth. Reflect weekly.

3 MONTHS
Read 1 book. Journal weekly. Block 1 hour per week for learning

Figure 7.8 **Wise section, Better Life, By Design Worksheet example**

Start by defining your long-term wisdom goal. This should reflect how you want to think, lead, or show up differently over time. For example: 'To become a better version of myself through intentional growth.' This kind of goal gives you direction. It helps you choose the right inputs and stay focused on the habits that grow you over time. Next, identify the actions and measures that will support your growth. These could include goals like reading specific books each quarter, engaging with mentors, setting aside dedicated time for structured learning, or teaching a concept to your team once per quarter. Use the worksheet to capture five to ten actions and track how you'll measure them. The key is to choose habits that suit your learning style and rhythm.

Once you've established the goal and actions, break them into time-based milestones. These should be clear, measurable steps that help you stay on track. Start with a 10-year goal that outlines your vision for wisdom.

Then break it down into a 3-year, 1-year, and 90-day goals, each one building toward that long-term vision. The Better Life, By Design worksheet helps you capture these milestones, aligning them with your long-term vision. Your goals should be personalised, reflecting your unique journey and definition of wisdom.

From the big picture to the next 90 days, you're designing a wisdom strategy that supports the life you want to create, intentionally and by design.

The Better Wisdom, By Design Assessment

Here are three questions to help you assess where you currently stand on wisdom in your Better Life, By Design. Reflect on each one and rate yourself honestly. This self-check will give you a clearer view of how well you're investing in your growth, and where small changes could multiply your long-term wisdom.

- *Have you clearly defined a personal wisdom goal, and would you confidently rate your progress toward it at 8/10 or higher?*

- *Are you consistently taking actions that grow your wisdom, and would you rate your consistency at 8/10 or higher?*

- *How well are you balancing the key levers of wisdom: curated learning, lived experience, and self-reflection and would you confidently rate that balance at 8/10 or higher?*

Wisdom is the quiet multiplier behind every other part of your life. It shapes how you lead, how you grow, and how you respond to everything life throws your way. When you grow wiser, everything else gets easier. Health improves. Wealth compounds faster. Relationships deepen. A wise life isn't something you stumble into. It's something you design. Now that you've built a clear plan to grow your wisdom with intention, it's time to turn to the next part of your journey: building a life where you feel truly happy, on purpose.

Happy

'Happiness and freedom begin with a clear understanding
of one principle: Some things are within our control, and some
things are not. It is only after you have faced up to this fundamental
rule and learned to distinguish between what you can and can't control
that inner tranquillity and outer effectiveness become possible.'
EPICTETUS

'Happiness is not a smiling face. It's a smiling soul.'
JONNY THOMSON

'If you were watching a movie about your life, what would you yell
at the screen to make you happier today?'

We often think of happiness as a reward at the end. Something we'll get once we hit a certain number, finish the project, or finally take that trip. But real happiness doesn't arrive after the credits. It's written into the story, moment by moment. And too often, we don't see the plot drift until we're already off course.

Happiness isn't just about how good life looks on the outside. It's about how it feels on the inside. It's the quiet contentment that comes from living with intention. It's the joy you feel when doing something that matters, surrounded by people who matter. It's the sense that you're on the right path, even if it's not always easy. When you're happy, you feel full. Not because everything is perfect, but because it's meaningful.

And yet, so many Owner Leaders trade it away. Not deliberately, but gradually and subtly. They postpone it. They say they'll be happy once they hit a number, sell the business, or finally take a holiday. But when they reach that point, something still feels missing. I've seen it time and again. Owners who have built incredible businesses yet feel quietly miserable. Not because they failed, but because they've been sprinting for so long that they forgot what the race was for.

You didn't build your business to feel stuck in it. You didn't chase success just to feel empty at the finish line. You built it because you believed it would create freedom and fulfilment. But those outcomes don't arrive by accident. They require design.

Long before the pressures of modern life, people asked the same question we still ask today: what does it truly mean to live well?

Across thousands of years and cultures, the world's greatest thinkers have wrestled with the question of happiness. And while their traditions differ, certain truths appear again and again in philosophy, religion, and even modern psychology. Happiness, in the end, is less about what you chase and more about how you choose to live.

Philosopher Jonny Thomson summarises these recurring themes as the three pillars of happiness:

- *First, happiness is not pleasure. It's purpose.*

The ancient Greeks called this *eudaimonia*—a life of flourishing. It's the kind of happiness you often realise in hindsight. You might not have felt 'happy' during the hard years of raising children or building your business, but you look back and recognise those were deeply fulfilling times. That's the kind of happiness we mean here: purpose-driven, not pleasure-driven.

- *Second, happiness is not found in extremes. It lives in moderation.*

Ancient traditions like Buddhism, Stoicism, and Daoism all teach the value of the middle way. In Owner Led Companies, we tend to swing between intensity and withdrawal, with periods of relentless overwork followed by stretches of disengagement, exhaustion, or retreat. But happiness thrives in rhythm, where there's time to build and time to breathe.

- *Third, happiness is tied to virtue. You can't be truly happy if you're ashamed of how you're living.*

Aristotle defined happiness as the result of living virtuously. It wasn't about feeling good, but about *being good*. You became happy by becoming excellent. By acting with courage, justice, and integrity. That idea is still powerful today, especially for Owner Leaders. Because when you live in a way that aligns with who you want to be, happiness isn't something you chase. It's something that follows.

As shown in Figure 7.9, happiness lives at the intersection of these three pillars: purpose, virtue, and moderation. Remove any one of them, and the foundation becomes unstable. But when all three are in balance, happiness isn't fleeting. It becomes durable and deeply felt.

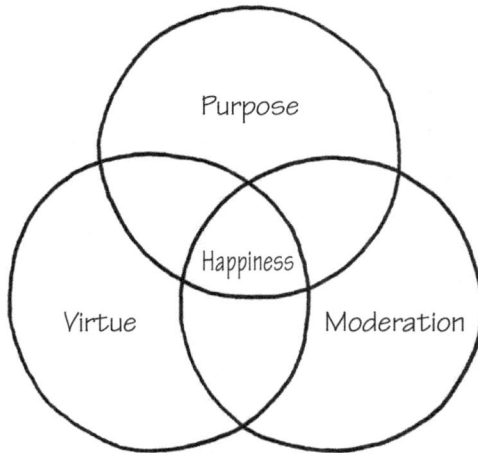

Figure 7.9 **The Three Pillars of Happiness**

If you cut corners, betray your values, or sacrifice what matters most, happiness will quietly withdraw. Living well requires that you're proud of how you lead. Happiness isn't just a feeling. It's a reflection of who you are.

That's why not all happiness is created equal. What many people experience as happiness is actually hedonia, a pursuit of short bursts of pleasure, relief, or escape. In Greek philosophy, hedonia is the kind of happiness tied to immediate gratification. Often, what people are chasing isn't happiness at all, but relief, relief from pressure, uncertainty, or the constant strain of running at full speed. When that pressure lifts briefly, such as after a deal closes, a problem is resolved, or a moment of stillness arrives, it can feel like happiness. But this type of happiness is fleeting, unstructured, and often accidental.

True happiness is different. It doesn't come from the absence of discomfort; it comes from the presence of alignment, when how you live reflects what matters most to you. In contrast to hedonia, eudaimonia is about long-term flourishing and the pursuit of a life lived with purpose. While hedonia offers brief relief, eudaimonia provides lasting fulfilment that's aligned with our deepest values and purpose.

Figure 7.10 compares these two types of happiness, hedonia and eudaimonia, and the role each plays in shaping how we experience joy, peace, and fulfilment.

HEDONIA	EUDAIMONIA
Short-term pleasure, often mistaken for happiness	*A meaningful life built through virtue and purpose*
• Pleasure-seeking	• Purpose-driven
• Short-term gratification	• Long-term fulfilment
• Emotion-focused	• Character-focused
• Avoidance of discomfort	• Growth through challenge
• Often passive consumption	• Active contribution

Figure 7.10 **Hedonia vs Eudaimonia**

The reward of true happiness is calm, clarity, and connection. It's waking up without dread, choosing how you spend your time, and deciding who you spend it with. It's knowing that, even in the mess of real life, you're building something that matters, not someday, but now.

And if you ignore it? You might still succeed. You might build a profitable company, but you risk losing your sense of self in the process. I once worked with an owner who sold their business for $30 million. Six months later, they told me, 'I thought I'd be happier.' It wasn't because they lacked options, but because they had lost their sense of purpose. Their business had been their identity. And with it gone, their joy disappeared too.

If something feels off, even if everything looks successful on paper, this is where it starts. Happiness doesn't come automatically; it's a conscious choice.

Just like your business, it improves with focus and structure. Happiness isn't a gift or a matter of luck, timing, or personality; it's a practice. That practice begins by getting clear on what happiness looks like for you, what gives your life meaning, what energises you, and what makes you feel most like yourself. When you put structure around those answers, happiness stops being accidental. It becomes something you can shape, sustain, and protect.

Now that you've explored what happiness really means, and how purpose, moderation, and virtue shape it, it's time to define your own version. Use the framework below to make happiness practical, not a vague idea but a lived experience. Think about the moments that lift you, the habits that keep you grounded, and the people who help you feel most like yourself.

Designing your Happy Life

The three pillars of purpose, moderation and virtue form the foundation of a life that feels meaningful, not just busy. Now it's time to translate that insight into structure.

By now, you've set goals for your health, wealth and wisdom. Now you'll do the same for happiness. Use the Better Life, By Design worksheet to define what happiness looks like for you, how you'll bring it to life, and what that looks like in action across the next 90 days.

Before you begin, take a moment to reflect on your version of eudaimonia: a life guided by purpose, shaped by moderation, and anchored in virtue. What would it feel like to live that way, consistently, intentionally, and on your terms?

In the Better Life, By Design worksheet, you'll define a goal that captures how happiness will be intentionally integrated into your life. Not as a vague feeling, but as a lived rhythm of time, energy, and presence. From there, you'll identify the actions and habits that support it, weekly commitments, personal boundaries, and meaningful time with the people and experiences that matter most. Figure 7.11 provides an example of how to bring this to life with clear, measurable goals that turn happiness into commitments you can track. Just as you've brought discipline to your business and finances, now you're doing the same for joy. From the big picture to the next 90 days, this is happiness by design.

Happy

OVERALL GOAL

To live a joyful and meaningful life, surrounded by people
I care about, doing what matters most

ACTIONS & MEASURES

Time spent with family or friends, habits that energise, experiences
that bring joy or calm, boundaries that protect your peace

10 YEAR

8 weeks off, 60 days per year with family / friends, 4 personal
trips per year. Maintain 3 weekly energetic, joyful habits

3 YEAR

6 weeks off, 36 days per year with family / friends,
3 personal trips per year

1 YEAR

5 weeks off, Start horse riding again, travel The Camino
de Santiago, Volunteer at school

3 MONTHS

1 full week, Quit the board work, Choose dates for Camino trip;
walk 100 km in training

Figure 7.11 **Happy section, Better Life, By Design worksheet example**

The Better Happiness, By Design Assessment

Here are three questions to help you assess where you currently stand on happiness in your Better Life, By Design. Reflect honestly on each one. This self-check is a chance to evaluate whether you're designing joy with intention or drifting toward a version of success that leaves fulfilment behind.

- *Have you clearly defined a long-term happiness goal, and would you confidently rate your progress toward it at 8/10 or higher?*

- *Are you consistently investing in the habits, relationships, and experiences that energise and ground you, and would you confidently rate that consistency at 8/10 or higher?*

- *How well are you balancing the three pillars of happiness—purpose, moderation, and virtue—to create a life that feels meaningful and alive, and would you confidently rate that balance at 8/10 or higher?*

Happiness is the emotional engine behind everything you're building. It fuels your energy, your presence, and your ability to stay grounded in what matters most. When you live with joy and alignment, everything else flows better. Work becomes more meaningful. Relationships become richer. Decisions become clearer. Happiness isn't at the end of the journey. It's what makes the journey worth taking. Now that you've built a clear plan to live with more joy, energy, and intention, it's time to turn to the people who matter most: the ones you call family.

Great Family

'Don't educate your children to be rich. Educate them to be happy,
so they know the value of things, not the price.'
VICTOR HUGO

You didn't build your business to disappoint the people you care about most. And yet, that's often the trade-off, because the pursuit of bigger consumes everything. One more deal. One more fire to put out. One more reason to say, 'Not now.' The business grows, but presence shrinks. And over time, the people you built everything for can feel like afterthoughts. Not because you don't care, but because you haven't designed a better way. A great family doesn't need perfection or constant proximity. It needs leadership. It needs intention. It needs protected time, real presence, meaningful traditions, and the courage to show up consistently. If you want to build a better life, you can't leave family to chance. You have to lead it on your terms, by design.

Family doesn't fall apart overnight. It drifts. The check-ins get shorter. The table gets quieter. The rituals fade without anyone deciding to end them. What once felt close becomes functional. Relationships shift into logistics: pick-ups, schedules, reminders. You're there, but not really. You're nodding, but not listening. Your kids stop bringing you the small things, so you miss the big ones too. And for Owner Leaders, that gap cuts especially deep, because it contradicts everything the business was supposed to support. You built it to support your family, not to step further from it. But when there's no structure, no rhythm, and no clear leadership at home, the drift becomes default. You still show up to the birthday, the holiday, the school event. But deep down, you know you're skimming the surface. And what you really wanted was something better, with connection, influence, and a family that gets stronger over time.

A great family doesn't just happen. It is shaped with intention, through the rhythms you protect and the leadership you provide. When family drifts, it is not because no one cares. It is because no one leads. Just as you have built rhythm and structure into your business, your family needs the same. These four levers form the foundation of a strong family life.

- *Family Leadership*

You're not the boss of your family, but you are its architect. Family leadership means showing up with intention, guiding values, modelling behaviour and maintaining the structure your family needs to thrive. That could mean initiating a family conversation about core values, organising the next gathering, or mentoring a child through a hard season. It's not about control. It's about responsibility.

- *Protected Time*

This is time you protect from work so it becomes part of your family's rhythm, not just what's left over. It's planned, consistent and honoured. It might be a standing Tuesday dinner with your partner, a no-phone Sunday afternoon with your kids, or setting aside a long weekend for extended family every quarter. Protected time gives family a visible, recurring place in your life, not just a hope but a habit.

- *Presence*

Just being physically present isn't enough. True presence means full attention and emotional availability. It looks like pausing a task to help with homework, listening without rushing to fix, or noticing the moment your child lights up about something they care about. Presence is not about grand gestures. It is about making the people around you feel seen, heard and important.

- *Family Traditions*

Traditions are how families build memory, identity and belonging. They can be weekly, like pancakes on Sunday morning. They can be annual, like a camping trip with cousins or a rotating holiday dinner. And they can be one-on-one, like a yearly father–daughter getaway or a birthday breakfast with each child. What matters is that they happen often enough to matter and intentionally enough to last.

Each of these levers supports the others. Protected time creates the space. Presence fills it with depth. Traditions give it rhythm. And leadership ties it all together. When you activate all four, something powerful happens. You don't just stay close; you grow closer. When you lead your family with care, these four elements begin to compound. They don't just hold your relationships together. They make them deeper, stronger and more meaningful over time.

Now it's time to turn that clarity into structure. This is how you become the architect of something that lasts, even beyond you. In the Better Life, By Design worksheet, you'll define what a great family looks like for you and how you'll bring it to life with intention.

Designing your Great Family Life

You've now seen what makes a family stronger over time: protected time, real presence, meaningful traditions, and intentional leadership. These are the design elements that bring connection, rhythm, and resilience to the people who matter most. Now it is time to turn that clarity into structure. In the *Better Life, By Design* worksheet, you will define what a great family looks like for you, the actions that will bring it to life, and the rhythms that will keep it growing. Figure 7.12 offers an example of how to translate your family vision into specific, measurable goals that reflect your values, relationships, and the legacy you want to build.

Start by defining your overall family goal, something that reflects the kind of relationships, rhythm, and impact you want to create within your family over time. For example one leader we worked with wrote: 'To build a strong, connected family that feels safe, supported, and deeply proud of who we are together.' This goal becomes your anchor, and it's timeless. It guides the decisions, habits, and commitments you will make to move from drift to design.

From there, define the habits and experiences that will bring that vision to life. These might include weekly dinners with your partner, one-on-one experiences with your children, or quarterly gatherings with extended family. You may choose to document shared values, create meaningful traditions, mentor younger family members, or participate in things that matter deeply to someone you love. Use the worksheet to list five to ten meaningful actions that will strengthen your family life. You might organise them by who they're for, how often they happen, or the kind of experience they create. The goal is not volume, but intentionality. Focus on the habits that matter most and that you can sustain over time.

Figure 7.12 shows an example of how to bring these elements together in a clear, structured format. Just as you've brought systems and clarity to your business, now you're doing the same for the people who matter most. From the big picture to the next 90 days, this is great family, by design.

Great Family

OVERALL GOAL

To build a strong, connected family that feels safe, supported, and deeply proud of who we are together.

ACTIONS & MEASURES

1:1 dinners, quarterly family gatherings, become a mentor to family members, document family values & create a calendar of traditions.

10 YEAR

Host 10 meaningful extended family gatherings, mentor 3 family members, and maintain at least 8 weeks of quality time each year with immediate family.

3 YEAR

Establish monthly rituals, plan 3 extended family events, document shared values, and complete one dedicated 1:1 experience with each child.

1 YEAR

Run 12 weekly family dinners, organise 4 one-on-one days with each child or partner, and lead planning for 2 milestone celebrations or family trips.

3 MONTHS

1 overnight trip with a loved one, host 1 extended family dinner or lunch, 3 weekly activities such as walks, shared meals, or unplugged time.

Figure 7.12 **Great Family section, Better Life, By Design Worksheet example**

The Better Great Family, By Design Assessment

Before you move on, take a moment to reflect on where your family life stands today. Are you showing up with intention, or just fitting people in around the edges? The questions below are designed to help you assess whether your family is being shaped by design or drifting in the margins of a busy life.

- *Have you clearly defined what a strong, connected family looks like for you, and would you confidently rate your progress toward that vision at 8/10 or higher?*

- *Are you consistently investing in the rhythms, relationships, and actions that strengthen your family, and would you confidently rate your habits at 8/10 or higher?*

- *How well are you balancing the core levers of family—protected time, presence, traditions, and leadership—and would you confidently rate that balance at 8/10 or higher?*

Family is where your leadership becomes most personal. Not because you hold authority, but because you shape the rhythm, the values, and the emotional safety of the people who matter most. When you bring structure to family with the same focus you apply to business, something changes. The home becomes a place where people feel connected, not just managed. Trust builds. Connection deepens. And the people you built everything for begin to experience the version of you that is present, intentional, and engaged, not the part that is stretched thin or distracted. That's when your business starts to support the life you truly want, a life that feels whole, grounded, and worth building well.

Next Steps

Thank you for reading *Bigger Isn't Better, Better is Better*.

This book was written to solve a specific problem. It's a problem that most Owner Leaders never fully name, but deeply feel. It's the constant pressure to grow, to chase more, to keep moving even when the payoff begins to shrink. That pressure distorts your priorities, your decisions, and the life you're building.

But here's the deeper truth: in an Owner Led Company, building a better business and building a better life are not two separate things. There's only one you. And if any part of your business is stuck in a doom loop, such as a misfiring team, disengaged customers, a struggling offering, or unstable financials, your life suffers too. When your personal life drifts, your business feels it. It shows up through distraction, fatigue, and reactionary decisions. These are not separate systems. It is one life, and if you do not lead both with intention, neither works the way you want.

Bigger Isn't Better is about offering a better alternative. One that prioritises clarity over chaos. One that builds momentum through rhythm, not just effort. One that helps you grow a business that serves your life, rather than consumes it.

Throughout this book, you've seen how drift happens. It creeps in quietly, gradually, and often with good intentions. It shows up in a culture that loses its soul, in customers who stop caring, in offerings that are easy to copy, and in finances that demand too much while delivering too little. These are not isolated problems. They are the symptoms of chasing growth without structure.

The four flywheels — Better Team, Better Customers, Better Offering, and Better Financials — are your counterforce. Together, they help you build a better business, not just a bigger one. And now, with the Better Life, by Design framework, you have the missing piece: a life structure to match your business strategy. One supports the other. That's the system you've built.

To give you the best chance to live it well and lead it confidently, consider the following best practices.

Begin at the Beginning

Start small. This book offers 35 questions, each one designed to help you spot drift, clarify your structure, and take action where it matters most. You're not meant to answer them all at once. Just pick the one that matters most right now.

Look through the questions from the four flywheels: Better Team, Better Customers, Better Offering, and Better Financials. Or explore the Better Life, by Design framework. Which one stands out? Which one feels most uncomfortable, most urgent, or most likely to create meaningful change if you addressed it?

Start with that question.

Use it to set a 90-day goal in your business or your life. Build the rhythm. Follow through. Then reassess.

The temptation will be to fix everything at once. But the power of this system is in the cycle. One question. One focus. One clear step forward. Let that build your new, better operating model, for both business and life.

Use Agendas

Every owner has good intentions. But without structure, intention fades. The best way to keep better alive is to build it into the rhythms you already run.

Whether it's your leadership team weekly, your monthly financial review, or your quarterly planning offsite, make time to check in on each flywheel and the questions that reveal how it's performing. Do the same with your personal worksheet. Review your five life domains at least once per quarter to stay aligned with your broader goals.

When better becomes part of your rhythm, it becomes part of your culture.

Use Data

You can't improve what you don't track. And in both life and business, the right measures reveal drift before it becomes damage.

In the business, measure what truly matters: retention, engagement, NPS, delivery margins or return on investment. Don't just focus on revenue. In your life, track progress across your goals for health, wealth, wisdom, happiness, and family. Whether it's hours protected, cash moved, books read, or meaningful time with the people who matter most, make your better version a measurable success.

Better isn't a feeling. It's a pattern you can see.

Use a Coach

The best Owner Led Companies don't try to do this alone. They build rhythms, execute strategy, and grow their teams with structure and external perspective. Not because they lack ability, but because they know that without support, drift always returns. And when it does, momentum stalls, culture frays, and progress becomes reactive instead of intentional.

That's the work we do every day at Evolution Partners. We help Owner Led Companies build better businesses. Ones that grow through clarity, structure, and discipline, not chaos.

We work with mid-sized firms across Australia and New Zealand to help them build better teams, better customers, better offerings, and better financials. Just as importantly, we help them design a better life that feels aligned, fulfilling, and worth building well.

Our certified coaches are based in regions across Australia and New Zealand, so support is close by and grounded in the realities of Owner Led Companies.

If you'd like to explore how this could work for you or talk through where to begin, I'd love to hear from you. You can reach me directly at brad.giles@evolutionpartners.com.au.

Tell me where you're headed, and let's build something better together.

If you're not ready for coaching but want to stay connected, I also publish a weekly newsletter and host a podcast focused on building better Owner Led Companies. Each week, I share practical ideas, tools, and interviews with leaders who are building businesses that work and lives that matter. You can subscribe or listen at *evolutionpartners.com.au*.

Use a Checklist

To help you apply the ideas in this book across both your business and your life, we've developed the Bigger Isn't Better Checklist. It brings together the key assessment questions from each chapter across Better Team, Customers, Offering, and Financials, as well as the life domains explored in the Better Life, by Design framework.

Use this checklist regularly—quarterly, annually, or as part of your planning rhythm—to track where drift may be creeping in and where structure needs to be reinforced. If you can't confidently rate each item at 8/10 or higher, that's your signal. That's where better begins.

You can find a printable version at *evolutionpartners.com.au*

Bigger Isn't Better Checklist

evolutionpartners

1 BETTER TEAM

- ☐ Does your hiring process ensure that you consistently recruit A players infused with passion, and would you confidently rate your process at 8/10 or higher?
- ☐ Do you actively filter for curious achievers—those who are both enquiring and responsible—when hiring to ensure they thrive in an Owner Led Company, and would you rate your process at 8/10 or higher?
- ☐ Do curious achievers feel deeply engaged and find it hard to quit, and would you rate your workplace at 8/1 0 or higher in this area?
- ☐ Are you leading a team with soul, where people feel lucky to be a part of the organisation, and would you rate your team culture at 8/10 or higher?

2 BETTER CUSTOMERS

- ☐ Are you intentionally improving the experience for existing customers in many small ways that competitors aren't, and would you rate your discipline at 8/10 or higher?
- ☐ Does your business regularly exceed customer expectations in a way that fosters emotional loyalty, and would you confidently rate this at 8/10 or higher?
- ☐ Do you understand why customers don't repurchase or refer, and would you rate your process for doing so at 8/10 or higher?
- ☐ Is your team focused on increasing LTV by deepening customer relationships rather than acquiring more, and would you rate your focus at 8/10 or higher?
- ☐ Do you consistently deliver on your promises to customers in a way that builds trust, and would you confidently rate this at 8/10 or higher?

3 BETTER OFFERING

- ☐ Is your offering truly unique, addressing customer problems in ways that competitors struggle to replicate, and would you confidently rate it at 8/10 or higher?
- ☐ Is your offering evolving consistently, to make it more valuable to your customers, and would you confidently rate your process at 8/10 or higher?
- ☐ Are you leveraging your company's strengths to focus on what you can be the best at, and would you confidently rate your strategy at 8/10 or higher?
- ☐ Does your offering meet your customers' needs more effectively than your competitors', and would you confidently rate this at 8/10 or higher?
- ☐ Are you deepening your offering's value over time rather than just adding features, and would you confidently rate this at 8/10 or higher?

4 BETTER FINANCIALS

- ☐ Do you treat money in the business as a resource to allocate with discipline, not a reward to spend, and would you rate your financial mindset at 8/10 or higher?
- ☐ Do you apply disciplined investment criteria—based on return, timing, and risk—rather than reacting to opportunities, and would you confidently rate that approach at 8/10 or higher?
- ☐ Do you have a clear and intentional system for deciding how much profit stays in the business, how much supports your lifestyle, and how much goes to external assets—and would you confidently rate that system at 8/10 or higher?
- ☐ Are your reinvestments strengthening the parts of the business that create long-term value—like your people, customers, and offerings—and would you confidently rate your focus at 8/10 or higher?
- ☐ Do you track whether previous reinvestments are delivering measurable returns, and would you confidently rate that discipline at 8/10 or higher?

5 BETTER HEALTH, BY DESIGN

- ☐ Have you clearly defined your long-term health goal, and would you confidently rate your progress toward that goal at 8/10 or higher?
- ☐ Are you consistently taking actions that support both your physical and mental endurance? Would you rate your consistency and follow-through at 8 out of 10 or higher?
- ☐ How well are you balancing physical endurance (exercise, nutrition, sleep) with mental endurance (purpose, social connection, anticipation), and would you confidently rate your balance at 8/10 or higher?

6 BETTER WEALTH, BY DESIGN

- ☐ Have you clearly defined your long-term personal wealth goal, and would you confidently rate your progress at 8/10 or higher?
- ☐ Are you consistently extracting surplus from the business and investing it wisely, using clear rules? Would you rate your focus on this at 8/10 or higher?
- ☐ How well are you actively balancing the key levers of personal wealth: growing assets, building income, managing cashflow, and controlling debt? Would you confidently rate that balance at 8 out of 10 or higher?

7 BETTER WISDOM, BY DESIGN

- ☐ Have you clearly defined a personal wisdom goal, and would you confidently rate your progress toward it at 8/10 or higher?
- ☐ Are you consistently taking actions that grow your wisdom, and would you confidently rate your consistency at 8/10 or higher?
- ☐ How well are you balancing the key levers of wisdom: curated learning, lived experience, and self-reflection and would you confidently rate that balance at 8/10 or higher?

8 BETTER HAPPINESS, BY DESIGN

- ☐ Have you clearly defined a long-term happiness goal, and would you confidently rate your progress toward it at 8/10 or higher?
- ☐ Are you consistently investing in the habits, relationships, and experiences that energise and ground you, and would you confidently rate that consistency at 8/10 or higher?
- ☐ How well are you balancing the three pillars of happiness—purpose, moderation, and virtue—to create a life that feels meaningful and alive, and would you confidently rate that balance at 8/10 or higher?

9 BETTER GREAT FAMILY, BY DESIGN

- ☐ Have you clearly defined what a strong, connected family looks like for you, and would you confidently rate your progress toward that vision at 8/10 or higher?
- ☐ Are you consistently investing in the rhythms, relationships, and actions that strengthen your family, and would you confidently rate your habits at 8/10 or higher?
- ☐ How well are you balancing the core levers of family—protected time, presence, traditions, and leadership—and would you confidently rate that balance at 8/10 or higher?

Need help? Visit www.evolutionpartners.com.au

Figure 7.13 **Bigger Isn't Better Checklist**

Enjoy the Journey

This is the part most owners miss.

They build the business. They chase the goals. They get the results. But they never stop to ask: is this the life I actually want?

Now you've asked it. And more than that, you've answered it.

You've defined what better means in your business and in your life. You've chosen structure over chaos, rhythm over reactivity, and intention over drift. That doesn't mean it will be perfect. But it means you're no longer guessing. You're leading with clarity.

So build with intent. Live fully. Celebrate what matters. And enjoy the journey, by design.